Steve Bucci's
Total Phillies Trivia

Camino Books, Inc.
Philadelphia

Manufactured in the United States of America

1 2 3 4 5 12 11 10 09

Library of Congress Cataloging-in-Publication Data

Bucci, Steve.
  Steve Bucci's total Phillies trivia / by Steve Bucci.
      p. cm.
    ISBN 978-1-933822-20-4 (alk. paper)
    1. Philadelphia Phillies (Baseball team)—Miscellanea. 2. Baseball—
Pennsylvania—Philadelphia—Miscellanea. I. Title.

    GV875.P45B83 2009
    796.357'640974811—dc22   2009010267

Cover and interior design: Jerilyn Bockorick

Cover photographs are reproduced from Rich Westcott, *The Fightin'
Phils: Oddities, Insights, and Untold Stories* (Camino Books, Inc., 2008).

This book is available at a special discount on bulk purchases for
promotional, business, and educational use.

Publisher
Camino Books, Inc.
P.O. Box 59026
Philadelphia, PA 19102

www.caminobooks.com

Contents

Preface

Broad Street is gone. You can't see it. Not the asphalt, not the traffic lines painted in white, not the sidewalks, none of it. I am looking at the photograph on the front page of the *Philadelphia Daily News* on November 1, 2008. It's a shot of South Broad from a high angle looking north to City Hall. In the photograph, Broad Street isn't a street, but a raging river of humanity. It's as if a tidal wave of red–clad Phillies fans has crashed into Center City and has flooded every inch of open space. In the photo the torrent of bodies is flowing south toward the Sports Complex. What the *Daily News* has captured for posterity is the scene shortly following the Phillies' 2008 Championship Parade. The procession of flat–bed trucks carrying the players has passed that point of the route, but now the fans are following it by the hundreds of thousands. They are walking behind it en masse, much like a golf tournament gallery follows Tiger Woods as he moves down a fairway. This is the strength of the bond between team and city. Especially this team, the 2008 team, that has broken the city's 25–year championship drought and the Phillies' 28–year World Series title drought. It proves that there is nothing trivial about the place the franchise holds in the hearts of Philadelphians.

Rewind now to a warm Sunday night in early September. The Phillies are playing the Mets at Shea Stadium. The pitching matchup is worth the price of admission alone. The Phils send young ace Cole Hamels to the mound. For the Mets, it's two–time Cy Young Award–winner Johan Santana.

It's on nights like this one that I'm reminded of why we love baseball so much. The thrill of the big game. The anticipation of what might be. The chance to experience something unforgettable. It's nights like these that produce the moments that we will remember for years to come. And as the years go by, those moments become the answers to trivia questions.

As I listen to the radio broadcast of the Phillies–Mets game, I wonder if anything from the game will turn into a future answer, even one that might find its way into the book you're now reading. And then it happens, third inning with Ryan Howard at the plate. The big slugger uncoils on a Santana pitch and delivers a mammoth home run. It's Howard's 40th of the season, and with it he becomes the first Phillie ever to have three consecutive 40–home–run seasons. (Remember that little nugget, because it will come up later in the book.)

In baseball, trivia matters. And it matters to the great baseball fans of Philadelphia. There has been many a night when I've walked into Downey's at the foot of South Street, and Tommy Brennan, baseball trivia maven, is tending bar. He'll greet me with a "Who holds the Phillies record for most scoreless innings by a reliever?" It's like Norm, in the TV series *Cheers*, being greeted as he walks in the door, only instead of being greeted by name, it's with a baseball trivia question. There's always at least a half dozen guys in on the action. The questions flow like the draft beer being drawn from the bar's taps. Who was the fifth starter on the '93 Phillies? Which pitchers named Jim have won the Cy Young Award? Name the active player who has over 1,000 hits with two different teams. It goes on and one until it's well past closing time and we're still trying to stump one another.

Here's one that usually gets people: Name the oldest continuous, one–name, one–city team in major league history. Give up? It's your own Philadelphia Phillies. They've lasted in this town for almost 130 years. The team is as synonymous with Philly as the Liberty Ball and the cheesesteak. Can you honestly imagine life without them?

In 2009, the Phillies turned 126. In their lifetime they've seen it all. Heartache and heartbreak, ups and downs, triumphs and tragedies, pennant race collapses, bumbling ballplayers, Hall of Fame immortals, colorful characters, controversial figures, the bizarre and off–the–wall, over 10,000 losses, and most of all, two glorious World Championships!

This book recounts much of that history. There are nearly 800 trivia questions and challenges in its 24 sections. While most of the book is in straight question form, there are a number of multiple–choice questions and match games. There is also a section of "Who Am I?" puzzles, similar to the scoreboard game played at Citizens Bank Park. Records are highlighted, including individual, team, single–game, single–season, and career. There are also sections that focus on the pennant–winning teams as well as the 1964 team, whose exploits turned out to be among the most trivial.

There is a section solely devoted to Mike Schmidt, who most would agree is the franchise's greatest player. Also, the managers, the owners, the all–stars, the award–winners, the quotable, the tradable, the postseasons, the weird and wild, and even the ballparks are among other categories in which you will be quizzed.

There is a section called "Whose Line Is It?" where you must determine the player who put up the statistical line in question, and in which season. You'll also find a match game of players' nicknames and a numbers game in which your knowledge of Phillies uniform numbers is tested.

My hope is that this book is not *too* challenging. The goal was not so much to make it hard as to make it interesting.

But my greatest hope is that you enjoy reading it as much as I enjoyed writing it.

1

Single-Season Feats

The Phillies franchise has existed since 1883, and over the years there have been many special moments. October 29, 2008, the night the Phils clinched their latest World Series title, ranks at the top. There have also been many single-season achievements that rate as special. Here are a few of those records, some of which stand as major league and National League marks. A few of the names, and feats, may have been long forgotten. Others will bring back special memories.

1. Who is the only Phillie to have 200 hits and 40 home runs in the same season?
2. What is the Phillies' single-season record for games played, and who holds it?
3. Which Phillie had the most hits in a single season?
4. Who holds the Phillies record for most home runs in a season? (If you don't know this one, you're an imposter as a Phils fan!)
5. Who holds the Phillies record for most home runs by a rookie?
6. Which Phillies pitcher hurled the most shutouts in a season?
7. Name the Phillie with the most stolen bases in his rookie season?
8. The pitcher who holds the Phillies' single-season record for wins is...? (This one goes way back.)

9. Which Phillies slugger holds the team record for strikeouts in a season?
10. Who holds the Phillies' single-season record for at-bats? (It's also the major league record.)
11. How about most at-bats by a right-handed hitter?
12. Most RBI in a season?
13. Most RBI by a right-handed hitter in a season?
14. Name the last Phillies catcher to hit 30 or more homers in a season.
15. Who was the first Phillie to notch at least 200 hits, 30 HRs, 20 triples, and 30 steals in the same season?

More Single-Season Feats

16. Who holds the Phillies' Spring Training HR record?
17. Which Phillie reached 60 RBI, the fastest in a season?
18. The Phillies' single-season record for strikeouts by a pitcher—who holds it?
19. Name the Phillie who was hit the most times by a pitch in one season.
20. Who was the last Phillies pitcher to win 20 games? (That's an easy one!)
21. The last "homegrown" starter to win 20 games? (That's a little tougher.)
22. The last time two Phillies starters won at least 17?
23. What is the Phillies' team record for consecutive losses?
24. Which pitcher homered in the most consecutive games? (His brother was a great hitter.)
25. Who holds the Phillies record for most grand slams in a season? (His brother was a great hitter, too!)
26. Name the Phillies pitcher with the lowest single-season ERA.
27. Which Phillies pitcher holds the team record for most games in a season?
28. Which batter struck out the most times in a season without hitting a home run?
29. Most at-bats by a pitcher who failed to get a hit?

Still More Single-Season Stuff

30. The team record for longest hitting streak is held by whom? And it's how many games? (Remember, the category is single-season.)
31. Who holds the Phillies record for most pinch hits by a rookie?
32. Name the last Phillie to lead the league in pinch hits?
33. Who holds the Phillies record for most pinch homers in a season?
34. Most strikeouts by a reliever in a season?
35. What is the largest deficit overcome by a Phillies team in September to win a division title?
36. Which Phillies team holds the franchise record for most losses in a season?
37. Which Phillie struck out the fewest times in a season (minimum 150 games)?
38. Who reached 20 HRs in a season faster than any other Phillie?
39. Who holds the Phils' record for most RBI by the All-Star Break?
40. Who is the last Phillie to homer in every ballpark in one season?

► **EXTRA BASE HIT**

Who holds the Phillies record for most pinch hits in a season?

ANSWERS

1. Hall of Famer Chuck Klein. In fact, he did it twice. In 1929, he had 215 hits and 43 homers, and followed that in 1930 with 250 and 40.
2. In 1979, the Phillies played 163 games, and Pete Rose played in them all.
3. Lefty O'Doul delivered 254 hits in 1929. But if he had gotten one more, he would've finished the year with a .400 average. Instead, Lefty had to settle for .398. He spent just two seasons with the Phils, but they were two of the best in team history. In '29, he also hit 32 homers and drove in 122. In 1930, his average "slipped" to .383.

4. Ryan Howard, who blasted 58 in his MVP season of 2006. That's 10 more than the previous record set by the great Mike Schmidt.

5. Willie Montanez hit 30 in his rookie year of 1971.

6. Grover Cleveland Alexander, 16 shutouts in 1916. It's a major league record that has little chance of ever being broken (although Dean Chance had 11 in 1964). Alex also won 33 games in '16.

7. Juan Samuel stole 72 when he was a rookie in 1984. It's also the club's single-season mark.

8. All the way back to 1890 when Kid Gleason won 38. Gleason later gained fame as the manager of the 1919 Black Sox. Alexander's 33 wins in '16 is the "modern record."

9. Ryan Howard, who whiffed a record 199 times in 2007. At the time, it was a new major league record. Howard matched that total again in 2008. But also in 2008, Arizona's Mark Reynolds struck out 204 times to break Howard's single-season record.

10. Jimmy Rollins had an amazing 716 at bats in 2007, which was an amazing season for J-Roll.

11. Juan Samuel holds the Phils' record by a righty with 701 in 1984.

12. Hall of Famer Chuck Klein's 170 in 1930. It's still the ML record by a lefty.

13. The club record by a righty belongs to Greg Luzinski, who knocked in 130 in 1977.

14. It's Mike Lieberthal, who went deep 31 times in 1999.

15. That would be . . . J-Roll, Jimmy Rollins, in 2007, who also became the first NLer with 20 doubles, 20 triples, 30 HRs and 30 steals since Willie Mays in 1957. Did I mention that '07 was an amazing season for J-Roll?

16. It's Ryan Howard, who hit 11 Grapefruit League homers in the spring of 2006. He never stopped hitting, all the way to an MVP season.

17. Michael Jack Schmidt needed just 70 games to reach 60 RBI in 1981. Hard to believe that this is the first time Schmidty's name has been mentioned in this section.

18. It's held by Curt Schilling. Schill was the top Phil on the hill in 1997, striking out an NL–best 319 batters. That eclipsed Steve Carlton's team record of 310. Carlton's total is the most by a Phillies left–hander.

19. His name is . . . Chase Cameron Utley. Chase was drilled 25 times in 2007.
20. Steve Carlton won 23 in 1982 to earn the last of his four Cy Young Awards.
21. The last "homegrown" starter, one developed in the Phillies' farm system, was Chris Short, who was a 20-game winner in 1966.
22. Carlton went 24-9, while Dick Ruthven was 17-10 in 1980. The Club's first championship season is the last to produce two starters with at least 17.
23. The answer to question 23 is 23. The Phils lost 23 in a row in 1961. That's the most in NL history, by the way.
24. Ken Brett homered in a major league record four consecutive starts in June 1973. Some think he was a better hitter than his brother, Hall of Famer George Brett.
25. No one's ever thought he was a better hitter than either of his brothers, but Vince DiMaggio holds the Phils' record for most grand slams in a season. Joe and Dom's big bro hit four in 1945.
26. It's Grover Cleveland Alexander. His ERA was 1.22 when he led the Phils to their first-ever pennant in 1915. Incredible when you consider he pitched at the hitter-friendly Baker Bowl.
27. Kent Tekulve pitched in 90 games in 1987.
28. The immortal Steve Jeltz had 0 HRs and 97 strikeouts in 1986.
29. Don Carmen had 31 at-bats in 1986 and failed to get a hit.
30. It's Jimmy Rollins' 36-game hitting streak in 2005. The streak reached 38 over two seasons. Utley had a 35-game streak in '06, the most by a lefty.
31. Mike Rogodzinski led the league with 16 pinch hits in his rookie season of 1973.
32. Greg Dobbs is the last Phillie to lead the league in pinch hits. Dobbs' 22 pinch hits led the majors in 2008.
33. Gene Freese hit five pinch home runs in 1959, his only season with the club.
34. The single-season record for strikeouts by a reliever is held by Dick Selma. Selma struck out 153 batters in a 134 innings in 1970.
35. Seven games with 17 to go. That was done by the 2007 Phils, who overtook a sputtering Mets team to win the NL East. Did it erase once and for all the stigma of '64?

36. The 1941 Phils lost a franchise record 111 games. How bad were they? The '41 Phils were so bad, they finished in eighth place, 57 games back! Heck, they were 19 games out of seventh. In one stretch, the '41 Phils were held scoreless for an unbelievable 28 innings in a row.

37. That was Emil Verban, who played second base for the Phils from 1946 to1948. In 1947, Verban played in all 155 games and whiffed only eight times—540 at-bats and eight strikeouts! He hit .285 that year.

38. No Phillie has gotten to 20 homers in a season faster than Chase Utley did in 2008. That season Utley reached the 20–homer plateau by June 1st.

39. It's Ryan Howard. In 2008, Howard had 84 RBI by the All-Star Break. He also had 28 home runs. Both marks were tops in the league. But, ironically, Howard did not make the NL All-Star team that season. It was the first time in 60 years that the league-leader in both categories was not a member of the NL squad.

40. Who else but the greatest home–run hitter in franchise history. Mike Schmidt homered in every ballpark during the 1979 season. He's the last Phillie to do so. Schmidty hit 45 dingers that year.

► EXTRA BASE HIT

It's Greg Dobbs, who broke Roy "Doc" Miller's record of 20 pinch hits last season. Dobbs had 22 in 2008. He eclipsed Miller with an RBI double on August 10th vs. Pittsburgh. The record-tying hit was a dramatic, three-run HR that capped a seven-run inning, and gave the Phils a come-from-behind 10-9 win over the Braves on July 26, 2008. In 2007, Dobbs led the league in pinch-hit RBI.

2

Single-Game Accomplishments

We all go to Phillies games hoping to see something we've never seen before. And, something we'll never forget. Each trip to the ballpark is filled with the anticipation and hope that one may see something historic. In some cases, it's historic because it's so futile. Maybe you witnessed first–hand one of the history–making performances recalled in this section.

1. We'll start with an easy one. What is the Phillies record for most home runs by a player in a single game?
2. What is the Phillies' team record for most home runs in a game
3. How about the Phillies' team record for most home runs in an inning?
4. Who holds the record for most home runs by an individual in a single inning?
5. What is the club record for most runs scored in a game (team)?
6. And the club record for most runs allowed in a game?
7. What is the club record for most hits in a game (team)?
8. Which player holds the record for hits in a game?
9. Who is the last Phillie to hit for the cycle?
10. Who is the last Phillie to hit an inside-the-park HR?

11. Who hit the last inside-the-park home run by a pitcher?
12. What is the Phillies record for longest extra-inning game?
13. How about latest ending game?
14. If you know the answer to 13, then do you recall the longest rain delay in Phillies history?
15. Who is the last Phillies pitcher to toss a no-hitter?
16. Who drove in the only run in the last Phillies no-hitter?
17. Who is the last left–hander to pitch a no-hitter for the Phillies?
18. Name the last Phillie to pitch a one-hitter.
19. Who is the only Phillie to steal second, third, and home in the same game?
20. Which Phillie holds the team record for most times hit by a pitch in a single game?
21 Name the only Phils pitcher to record a perfect inning (three strikeouts on nine pitches)?
22. Which Phillies pitcher struck out the most batters in a game?
23. Which Phillies pitcher holds the record for most strikeouts by a left-hander?
24. What do Gavvy Cravath, Willie Jones, Mike Schmidt, and Jayson Werth all have in common?
25. Who is the last Phillie to hit an "ultimate" grand slam (game-winner when trailing by three runs in the final inning)?

▶ EXTRA BASE HIT

Who turned the only unassisted triple play in Phillies history?

ANSWERS 1. The Phillies record is the same as the major league record: four homers in one game. Three of the franchise's all-time greats share the mark. It was first set by Ed Delahanty on July 13,1896, in a 9-8 loss to the Chicago White Stockings in Chicago. "Big Ed" became the second player in baseball history to hit four home runs in one game. He also had a single and six RBI. On July 10, 1936, Chuck Klein matched the feat in a 10-inning game at Pittsburgh's Forbes Field. Klein's fourth, in the top of the 10th, was the difference in a 9-6 Phillies win. Forty years later, Mike Schmidt joined

them in the record books. On April 17, 1976, in a wild, 10–inning affair vs. the Cubs at Wrigley Field, Schmidty hit four homers in four consecutive at-bats. Schmidt's final blast, a three–run shot, gave the Phils an 18-16 victory. Schmidt also tied another club record that day with eight RBI.

2. The Phillies as a team once hit seven home runs in a game. They did it on September 8, 1998. At the Vet, vs. the Mets. After all, one might expect something crazy to happen on 9/8/98. This was pretty crazy. Especially when you consider that Kevin Sefcik, of all people, went deep twice. That gave him three in 104 games on the season. Rico Brogna and Bobby Estalella also each hit two. Marlon Anderson capped it with a pinch-hit, two-run shot in the seventh. When the smoke cleared, the Phillies had a 16-4 win.

3. You think seven in a game is crazy? How about five in a single inning! June 2, 1949, vs. the Reds at Shibe. The Phils hit five home runs in a 10-run eighth inning. They trailed 3-2 and had only four hits heading into the bottom of the eighth. They ended up winning 12-3. Del Ennis, Andy Seminick, Willie Jones, and pitcher Schoolboy Rowe all went yard. One of them hit two out in that inning. He's the answer to the next question.

4. Andy Seminick and Von Hayes both hit two home runs in one inning. Seminick's two came in the aforementioned 10-run eighth vs. Cincinnati in '49. Seminick had three that day. Hayes hit a pair of first–inning homers vs. the Mets on June 11, 1985. Hayes was the first player in Major League Baseball history to homer twice in the first inning of a game. He led off the game with a solo homer off Tom Gorman. Then, with two outs in the inning, and Calvin Schiraldi on in relief, Hayes hit a grand slam. The Phils, with a nine-run first, were on their way to a 26-7 victory.

5. The 26 runs scored in the Von Hayes two–homer, first–inning game are the most runs scored by a Phillies team. Not only did they put a nine on the board in the first, but added seven in the second, five in the fifth, and four more runs in the seventh.

6. The Phillies once allowed 28 runs in a game. On July 6, 1929, the St. Louis Cardinals beat the Phillies 28-6 in the second game of a doubleheader.

7. The modern record (since 1900) is 27. The Phillies banged out 27 hits in that infamous 26-7 win over the Mets in '85. Juan Samuel went 5–for–7 to lead the way. The 1930 Phils also had a 27–hit game vs. the Pirates.

8. Connie Ryan got six hits at Pittsburgh on April 16, 1953, the most by a Phillie in a single game. Ryan delivered four singles and two doubles in a 14-12 Phillies loss. An infielder, he batted .257 in two seasons as a Phillie.

9. The last Phillie to hit for the cycle was David Bell. The third baseman notched the cycle in a June 28, 2004 game against the Montreal Expos. Bell went 4-for-4 with a walk, and drove in six runs. First he got the double, followed by a home run and a single. Bell completed the cycle with a seventh–inning triple.

10. Jimmy Rollins, on April 7, 2007 at the Florida Marlins. It was Rollins' third career inside the parker, and it came off his boyhood buddy, Dontrelle Willis.

11. The last Phillies pitcher to hit an inside-the-park HR was Curt Simmons. He hit it vs. Pittsburgh on May 22, 1952. It was the only HR of Simmons' career. On the mound he shut-out the Pirates 6-0.

12. The longest extra-inning game in Phillies history went 21 innings. It was a 2-1 loss at Chicago on July 7, 1918.

13. At 4:40 a.m. That's what time the second game of a doubleheader with San Diego ended on July 3, 1993. The doubleheader began on July 2nd. It is the latest a game has ended in MLB history.

14. That doubleheader ended at 4:40 a.m., thanks to three rain delays that totaled five hours and 54 minutes during game one. It was July 2, 1993 vs. San Diego. The delays lasted 1:10, 1:56, and 2:48. The game didn't end until one a.m. The Phils lost 5-2. But they won the early–morning "night-cap" in 10 innings, 6-5.

15. The Phillies' last no-hitter was tossed by Kevin Millwood. Millwood no-hit the Giants on April 27, 2003 at Veterans Stadium. The 29–year–old righty struck out 10, including Barry Bonds, while walking three. The final score was 1-0, Phils. It was the highlight of the Vet's final season, and certainly the highlight of Millwood's tenure as a Phil. After going 18-8 with the Braves in 2002, he was shipped to the

Phillies in exchange for a young catcher, Johnny Estrada. He lasted only two seasons in Philadelphia. Millwood was 14-10 with a 4.01 ERA in '03, but won just nine games the following season and signed with Cleveland as a free agent.

16. All of the offense in Millwood's no-hitter was provided by Ricky Ledee. And he did it with one swing. Ledee's solo homer in the bottom of the first inning accounted for the game's only run. That was plenty for Millwood on that day, as he turned in the ninth no-no in Phillies history. Ledee also made a diving catch to help preserve it.

17. The last left–hander to throw a no-hitter was Terry Mulholland. Mulholland's was the very first no-hitter at Veterans Stadium. It came on August 15, 1990, and like Millwood's, it came against the Giants. This one was an E-5 from being a perfect game. A seventh–inning throwing error by third baseman Charlie Hayes gave San Francisco its only base runner. Mulholland struck out eight, and didn't walk a single batter. He also hit an RBI single. Darren Daulton paced the Phillies at the plate with a two-run HR. The final score was 6-0. Afterward Mulholland quipped, "I had somebody else's slider."

18. Randy Wolf owns the franchise's last one-hit shutout. Wolfie one-hit the Reds on September 26, 2001. He gave up a single to the second batter of the game, Raul Gonzalez, then held them hitless the rest of the way. The Phillies won the game 8-0, as Wolf struck out eight, including Ken Griffey Jr. twice. It was his second career shutout, and the first Phillies one-hitter since Curt Schilling threw one in 1992.

19. Juan Samuel is a good guess. So is Jimmy Rollins, or perhaps Bob Dernier. But the correct answer is Pete Rose. Not only did he steal second, third, and home in the same game, he did it in the same inning. It was May 11, 1980 at Cincinnati. In the seventh inning with the Reds' Mario Soto on the mound, Rose coaxed a lead-off walk. Charlie promptly hustled to second, then stole third, and then, with Greg Luzinski at the plate, Rose stole home. The Phillies won the game, 7-3.

20. Chase Utley holds the record for most times hit by a pitch in a single game. Utley got plunked three times in an April 8, 2008 game against the Mets at Shea Stadium. Mets starter Oliver Perez hit Utley twice. Scott Schoeneweis drilled him again in

the seventh inning. Utley later scored in the inning and the Phillies went on to win it, 5-2.

21. The perfect inning is a baseball rarity. In 126 seasons, the Phillies have seen it accomplished only once. That was by Andy Ashby. It occurred in the fourth inning vs. the Reds at the Vet on June 15, 1991. Ashby set down Hal Morris, Todd Benzinger, and Jeff Reed swinging on three pitches each. Too bad Ashby gave up a two-run homer to Barry Larkin in the third inning. He lost the game, 3-1.

22. Art Mahaffey holds the Phillies record for most strikeouts in a nine-inning game. Mahaffey whiffed 17 Cubs on April 23, 1961 in the second game of a doubleheader at Connie Mack Stadium. Mahaffey matched what was then the NL record. Chris Short once struck out 18 Mets in 15 innings on October 2, 1965 at Shea Stadium. It was also in the second game of a doubleheader, a game which lasted 18 innings. The game was in a scoreless tie when it was eventually stopped by a one a.m. curfew.

23. Short, a lefty, owns the extra–inning mark with his 18–strikeout performance. But *the* lefty, Steve Carlton, holds the record for a nine–inning game. Carlton struck out 16 Cubs on June 9, 1982. Thanks to the 16–strikeout effort, he won a matchup with future Hall of Famer and ex-Phillie Ferguson Jenkins. It was an especially tough day for another future Hall of Famer and ex-Phil: Ryne Sandberg whiffed four times. Bill Buckner and Gary Woods were the Cubs' only starting position players not to strike out. In fact, they both went 3-for-3 with Woods drilling an HR. Carlton even got his former teammate Larry Bowa once. He gave up 10 hits, but walked only two to go along with the 16 strikeouts. The final was 4-2, Phillies.

24. They, along with Kitty Bransfield, share the Phillies record for most RBI in a game with eight. Schmidty drove in eight in his four–homer game in 1976, which was a 10–inning affair. Werth hit three home runs, including a grand slam, in his eight–RBI game in 2008 vs. Toronto.

25. The last "ultimate" grand slam was hit by Bo Diaz vs. the Mets on April 13, 1983. Down three, two out in the bottom of the ninth, bases loaded, and Diaz takes reliever Neil Allen deep. Diaz's grand slam gives the Phils a 10-9 victory. It was the ultimate. It was an ultimate grand slam!

► EXTRA BASE HIT

The answer is Mickey Morandini. On September 20, 1992 at Pittsburgh's Three Rivers Stadium: The Pirates' Jeff King nails a liner to Morandini. The Phillies' second baseman steps on the bag to retire Andy Van Slyke, then tags out Barry Bonds. Can't you just hear Harry Kalas? "Unassisted triple play, Mick-eee Mor-an-deee-neee!!" The only unassisted triple play in Phillies history.

3

Career Records

Some of the greatest careers of all time have been played out in Phillies pinstripes. In fact, 34 ex-Phillies have earned plaques in Cooperstown. Others, while not of Hall of Fame caliber, were very good in their own right. All have gone down in franchise history, as their exploits fill the franchise's record book.

Outlined here are questions pertaining to the club records, both individual and team.

1. Who is the Phillies' career leader in games played?
2. Who is the Phillies' career leader in at-bats?
3. Who is the Phillies' career leader in hits?
4. Here's an easy one. It's the one question that every Phillies fan is guaranteed to know. Who is the Phillies' all-time leader in home runs?
5. If you know that one, then you should know this one. Who is the Phillies' all-time leader in RBI?
6. This one's not as easy as the previous two (or five, for that matter). Who is the Phillies' all-time leader in doubles?
7. Who is the Phillies' all-time leader in slugging percentage?
8 Who hit the most singles in Phillies history?
9. Who holds the career record for pitching victories?
10. Which pitcher holds the Phillies' career record for complete games?

More Career Records

11. Which Phillies pitcher holds the major league record for most home runs allowed in a career?
12. Which Phillies pitcher had the most balks?
13. Who holds the Phillies record for career victories by a relief pitcher?
14. Who pitched the most career one-hitters in Phillies history?
15. Name the pitcher who suffered the most losses in team history.
16. Who is the youngest Phillie in team history to reach 100 RBI in a season?
17. How about fastest to reach 100 career home runs?
18. Who holds the Phillies' career record for home runs by a shortstop?
19. Who holds the Phillies' career record for home runs by a second baseman?
20. Who holds the Phillies' career record for home runs by a catcher?

Even More Career Records

21. Who holds the Phillies' all-time HR mark by a left–handed hitter?
22. Who holds the Phillies' career record for most home runs by an outfielder?
23. Who holds the Phillies record for most career hits by a switch hitter?
24. We know that Mike Schmidt is the Phillies' all-time HR king. But who is number two?
25. Which Phillie was caught stealing the most times in franchise history?
26. Which Phillie is the club's all-time leader in stolen bases? (Hint: Unless you're about 120 years old, you never saw him play.)
27. Who is the Phillies' all-time leader in pinch hits?

28. Two Phillies pitchers share the franchise record for most career home runs by a pitcher. Who are they?
29. Which Phillies pitcher made the most career starts?
30. Which Phillies pitcher struck out the most batters?

Still More Career Records

31. Which Phillie holds the team record for most times hit by a pitch?
32. Which Phillie holds the team record for most career grand slams?
33. How about most career inside-the-park home runs?
34. Who holds the Phillies record for most home runs in a single month?
35. Who holds the record for most RBI in a single month?
36. Who has hit the most extra-inning home runs in Phillies history?
37. Who has the highest career batting average in Phillies history?
38. Who is the Phillies' career saves leader?
39. Which Phillies pitcher has thrown the most wild pitches?
40. Which Phillie has hit the most career lead-off home runs?

▶ EXTRA BASE HIT

What is the Phillies' team record for most victories in a season?

ANSWERS 1. Michael Jack Schmidt played in 2,404 games in his illustrious Phillies career, the most in team history.
2. Same as above: Michael Jack, with 8,352 at-bats.
3. Ditto: Michael Jack with 2,234. Just 17 more hits than Richie Ashburn, who is second on the all-time list. Ashburn is the Phillies' all-time hits leader among left–handed batters

4. If you don't know that it's Michael Jack Schmidt, then you are a fradulent Phillies fan. Schmidty went "outta here" 548 times. When he retired, Schmidt ranked seventh on baseball's all-time HR list.

5. I promise that Mike Schmidt is not the answer to every question in this section, but he is the answer to this one. Schmidt's 1,595 RBI are tops in team history, and nearly 300 more than the next player on the list, Ed Delahanty.

6. He didn't have as many homers as Schmidt, but he had more doubles. Ed Delahanty hit 432 doubles as a Phillie, the most in franchise history.

7. Chuck Klein's .553 slugging percentage is tops in team history. (Schmidt is only third of all time.) Richie Allen is second and highest among right–handed hitters at .530.

8. Richie Ashburn hit the most singles in Phillies history. Whitey rapped out 1,811 in his Hall of Fame career as a Fightin' Phil.

9. Arguably the greatest pitcher in Phillies history, Steve Carlton. Carlton won 241 games in a Phillies uniform.

10. Hall of Famer Robin Roberts, who went the distance 272 times. Many argue that he is the greatest pitcher in Phillies history. (Let the debate rage over him, Carlton, and Grover Alexander.) The majority of Robin's career starts were complete games. How many guys can say that today? How many guys have any complete games today? Robbie even had an astounding streak of 28 *in a row!*

11. Robin Roberts surrendered 505 home runs. But that didn't stop him from winning 286 games in a career that led to the Hall of Fame.

12. Steve Carlton is the leader in balks. Carlton balked 90 times, which is not only a Phillies career record, it's the major league record. But that didn't stop him from winning 329 games in a career that led to the Hall of Fame.

13. It's not Tug McGraw. It's not Jim Konstanty. It's not Rheal Cormier. The correct answer is Ron Reed, who won 54 games in relief. Reed's career as a Phillie stretched from 1976 to 1983.

14. That's Steve Carlton, who never pitched a no-hitter, but tossed six one-hitters, the most in franchise history.

15. Would you believe Robin Roberts? He won 234 as a Phillie, the second most inteam history, but he also lost 199.

And that leads the franchise's all-time list. Carlton is second with 161, the most by a lefty.

16. Scott Rolen was 23 years old when he knocked in 110 in 1998. He's the youngest player in club history to have a 100–RBI season.

17. It took Ryan Howard just 325 career games to reach the 100–HR plateau. That's a major league record. Howard eclipsed Ralph Kiner's record of 385 games.

18. Jimmy Rollins is the number–one power–hitting shortstop. He finished the 2008 season with 125.

19. Chase Utley is already the all-time HR leader among Phillies second basemen. He passed Juan Samuel's previous record of 90 in 2007, Utley's fifth season.

20. Mike Lieberthal is the Phillies' all-time HR leader among catchers. "Liebie," who played 13 seasons with the Phils, blasted 149. He's also the Phils' leader in career games caught with 1,139.

21. It's Hall of Famer Chuck Klein, who clouted 243 in three tours of duty with the Phillies.

22. That would be Del Ennis. The native Philadelphian hit 257 of his 259 while playing both right and left fields in his 11 seasons as a Phillie.

23. Larry Bowa has the most hits among Phillies switch hitters. Bowa had 1,798 hits as a Phillie, fifth on the club's all-time list.

24. Number two is Del Ennis. The top home run–hitting outfielder in franchise history is second behind Schmidt. He's a distant second with 259, but only Schmidt has more. Ennis is also one of the top run–producers in Phillies history, ranking third of all time with 1,124 RBI.

25. Larry Bowa, who was caught stealing 94 times. (He was successful 288 times.)

26. Sliding Billy Hamilton swiped 508 bases from 1890 to1895. Hamilton was one of the greatest base stealers in the history of the game. He stole 912 in his career. Only Rickey Henderson and Lou Brock have more. Hamilton's season high of 115 in '91 is still the Phillies' all-time (pre-1900) single-season record.

27. Greg Gross, the most prolific pinch hitter in team history. Gross delivered 117 base hits in the pinch, more than double

the total of the next closest Phillie on the list. Gross was a solid utility player, but was a great pinch hitter and was frequently called upon. At the time of his retirement in 1989, his 588 pinch–hit at–bats were the most in baseball history. His 143 career pinch hits placed him third on the all-time list.

28. They are: Larry Christenson and Rick Wise. Each hit 11, the most of all time among Phillies pitchers. Wise, of course, is famous for hitting two during his no-hitter in 1971.

29. Steve Carlton would be the correct answer. Lefty went to the mound 499 times as a Phillie. Robin Roberts made the most starts by a righty with 472.

30. The same guy who made the most starts and had the most wins: Steve Carlton. Lefty whiffed 3,031 batters. His overall career mark of 4,136 is fourth of all time, and he was the first left–hander in baseball history to strike out 4,000.

31. It's Mike Lieberthal, who was plunked 88 times in his 13 seasons as a Phillie.

32. Mike Schmidt hit more grand slams than any other Phillie in team history. Schmidty went deep with the bases loaded seven times. That's one more than Bobby Abreu, Willie Jones, Chuck Klein, and Cy Williams.

33. Sherry Magee, who played in the early 20th century. Magee hit 19 inside–the–park homers in an 11–year career as a Phillie. He later played for the 1919 Cincinnati Reds, who beat the Black Sox in the World Series.

34. That record is shared by Jim Thome and 1920s–era slugger Cy Williams, who both hit 15. Williams hit 15 home runs in May 1923, while Thome equaled the mark in June 2004.

35. The same month he hit 15 homers in May 1923; Cy Williams knocked in 44 runs. That's still the highest total by a Phillie in a single month.

36. Who else but Mike Schmidt. If it's a home run record, Schmidt holds it. The Phillies' greatest home run hitter blasted nine in extra innings in his career.

37. Billy Hamilton hit .360 as a Phillie, the highest career mark in the franchise's history. For his 13-year career, the Hall of Famer hit .344. That ties him with Ted Williams, and is the fifth highest batting average in baseball history.

38. If you said Tug McGraw, you're wrong. Mitch Williams? No. Not even Steve Bedrosian. Would you believe it's Jose Mesa?

The one and only Joe Table saved 112 games, the most by a Phillie.

39. It's not the "Wild Thing," but "Lefty." Steve Carlton uncorked the most wild pitches—120.

40. That Phillie is Jimmy Rollins. He has opened a game for the Phillies with a home run 26 times. Like his boyhood hero, Rickey Henderson, who holds the major league record, Jimmy relishes the lead-off HR.

▶ EXTRA BASE HIT

A total of 101 victories is the most by any Phillies team, and that number has been reached twice in team history. The Phils won 101 in 1976, and again in 1977. Both teams won the NL East but lost in the League Championship Series. Some in the Phillies organization feel that the '77 team may have been the franchise's best ever. Conversely, the 1941 team was not. It holds the record for most losses with 111.

4

The Early Years

The Phillies have been around for a long time. Not surprisingly, as the years have passed, the first several decades of Phillies history have faded into the archives. As we watch from the 21st century, it's easy to overlook the contributions of the players who helped establish the Phillies as a cornerstone of the National League.

In this section, "the early years" are defined as those years ranging from the Phillies' inception in 1883 through the 1930s. Now I realize that covers about 56 years, which is almost half the team's existence. But let's face it, most of today's Phillies fans are under the age of 70. They've never heard of many of the names mentioned below, let alone be able to answer any of these questions.

So this is a section for the old-timers, and for those of you who possess an appreciation for early-era baseball. For the rest of you, consider this a learning tool—a reference guide to the early history of the Phillies. Read and learn about some terrific players, especially the ones who won the NL pennant in 1915, one of the greatest teams in Phillies history.

1. Who was the Phillie who hit what was then baseball's all-time single-season record of 24 home runs in 1915?
2. Name the three Hall of Famers who played together in the same Phillies outfield.
3. Which Phillies pitcher tossed four one-hitters in 1915?

4. Who was the winning pitcher in Game 1 of the 1915 World Series?
5. Who pitched the Phillies' first-ever no-hitter?
6. What was Ed Delahanty given by management as a gift for hitting four home runs in one game?
7. This Phillie was the first National Leaguer to hit 20 home runs in a season.
8. Who is the only Phillie to win the Triple Crown?
9. In what year did he accomplish the Triple Crown?
10. In 1894, this Phillie scored 196 runs, which still stands as baseball's all-time, single-season record.
11. Which Phillie won the 1910 batting title with a .331 average?
12. Name the Phillie who led the NL in home runs three times in the 1920s.
13. Which early-era pitcher twice lost 20 games for the Phillies, but became a Hall of Famer after being traded away?
14. What rival league lured away many early-era Phillies players with more lucrative contracts?
15. How many winning seasons did the Phillies enjoy during the decade of the 1930s?

► EXTRA BASE HIT

What team was disbanded and moved to Philadelphia by the National League, thus creating a new team called the "Phillies"?

ANSWERS

1. That Phillies name is Gavvy Cravath. He hit a whopping 24 homers in '15 to pace the Phillies to the NL pennant. That many homers in a season was an unheard–of total. But the record stood for just four years. That's when a guy named Babe Ruth clouted 29 in 1919. Cravath was Babe before Babe was Babe, leading the NL in home runs six times.

2. That's the trio of Ed Delahanty, Billy Hamilton, and Sam Thompson, who played the outfield for the Phillies from 1891 to 1895. All three players are enshrined in Cooperstown. In 1894, they combined for a .400 average. Thompson hit .404,

Delahanty .400, and Hamilton .399. No outfield combination in baseball history has ever hit for a higher average.

3. The man named after a president, Grover Cleveland Alexander. The one-hitters were four of Alex's 31 victories in 1915. The last of the four clinched the franchise's very first pennant. Alexander's 31 wins led the league. His 241 strikeouts and 1.22 ERA were also tops in the NL.

4. Grover Cleveland Alexander, who beat the Red Sox 3-1 in the opener. But the Phillies lost the next four, and didn't win another World Series game until 1980. For 65 years, Alexander held the distinction of being the only Phils hurler with a World Series victory.

5. Charlie Ferguson pitched the Phillies' first-ever no-no in 1885. From 1884 to 1887, Ferguson won 99 games and is widely regarded by historians as the franchise's first superstar. But Ferguson died tragically of typhoid fever in 1888. He was only 25.

6. When Delahanty homered four times in one game, it was only the second time in baseball history that the feat had been achieved. Even the opposing pitcher who surrendered the fourth shot met Delahanty at the plate to congratulate him. The Phillies thought so much of the accomplishment that they presented Big Ed with four boxes of chewing gum! One for each round-tripper.

7. Sam Thompson crushed 20 dingers in 1889. No other Phillie that season reached double figures in home runs. The next closest on the list was third baseman Joe Mulvey, who had six.

8. Chuck Klein is the only Phillie to lead the league in batting average, HRs, and RBI in the same season, one of only four National Leaguers to do so.

9. Klein did it 1933 when he hit .368, with 28 homers and 120 RBI. Despite Klein's heroics, the Phillies lost 92 games in '33 and finished in seventh place, 31 games back. Interestingly, that same year, Jimmie Foxx of the A's won the Triple Crown in the AL. How amazing is that? Triple Crowns were won in both leagues, and in the same city!

10. That would be Billy Hamilton, the fleet-footed Hall of Fame outfielder.

11. Sherry Magee, who was the first Phillies batting champ of the "modern" era (since 1900). Hamilton led the league in 1891 to capture the Phillies' first-ever batting title.
12. The answer is Cy Williams. He led the league in '20 with 15, in '23 with 41, and in '27, at the age of 40, he tied for the lead with 30.
13. His name is Eppa Rixey. The left-handed pitcher went 87-103 in eight seasons with the Phillies. Traded to the Reds in 1920, Rixey averaged 20 wins a season in his first five in Cincinnati. When his career was over, Rixey had 266 victories. At the time, that was the most among lefties. In 1963, he was elected to the Hall of Fame by the Veterans Committee.
14. The Federal League was that rival.
15. One in 1932, when they went 78-76 to finish fourth. Four times in the '30s, they lost over 100 games; twice they lost over 90. The 1939 Phillies went 45-106, and finished a whopping $50^1/_2$ games out of first place.

▶ EXTRA BASE HIT

That team was the Worcester Brown Stockings. National League president A.G. Mills thought he needed a team in Philadelphia, which at the time was a major population center. He awarded the franchise to Al Reach, the team's first owner, and the Phillies were born.

5

1950

The 1950 Phillies, the beloved "Whiz Kids," captured the hearts and imaginations of an entire generation of Philadelphians. Their thrilling run to the National League pennant is a central part of the city's sports lore. And the heroes of that wonderful summer are still deeply woven into the fabric of that era in Philadelphia. How much do you know, or remember, about the "Whiz Kids"?

1. Who coined the term "Whiz Kids"?
2. Who was the captain of the 1950 Phillies?
3. Who was the highest–paid player on the 1950 Phillies?
4. Who was the starting catcher on the 1950 Phillies?
5. What team did the Phillies beat in the final game of the season to clinch the NL pennant in 1950?
6. Who was the opposing pitcher and eventual loser of that game?
7. Whom did Richie Ashburn throw out at the plate in that final game of the '50 season?
8. Who started the Phillies' game-winning rally in the final game of the '50 season?
9. Which Phillie hit the game-winning home run to clinch the pennant in '50, and in what inning did he hit it?
10. How many runs scored on that game-winning and pennant-clinching HR?

More "Whiz Kids" Trivia

11. How many innings did Phillies starter Robin Roberts pitch in the pennant-clinching win?
12. How many victories did Robin Roberts have in 1950?
13. How many games did Jim Konstanty save in 1950?
14. Who led the '50 Phillies in home runs and RBI?
15. Who had the highest batting average on the '50 Phillies?
16. Who led the '50 Phillies in triples?
17. Who was the catcher who applied the tag on Ashburn's famous throw home in the final game of the '50 regular season?
18. In a game vs. the Giants in August 1950, which Phillie ignited a bench-clearing brawl that required the police to help restore order?
19. Which "Whiz Kid" was the son of a Hall of Fame great?
20. Who was the manager of the "Whiz Kids"?

▶ EXTRA BASE HIT

Which "Whiz Kid" was named Most Valuable Player in the National League?

ANSWERS

1. A New York City sportswriter named Harry Grayson is thought to have come up with the moniker.

2. Shortstop Granny Hamner was the captain of the 1950 team. Despite being only 22 years old when the season started, "Ham" was a feisty leader, and the backbone of the "Whiz Kids." He was signed in 1944, right out of high school at age 17, and immediately joined the big league club. In '50, Hamner batted .270, and drove in 82 runs, one of his better seasons at the plate.

3. Robin Roberts, whose salary, according to Baseball-reference.com, was $50,000 in 1950. And he was worth every penny that year, establishing himself as the staff ace, and one of the best pitchers in the National League.

4. Andy Seminick was the starting catcher on the 1950 Phillies. At age 30, Seminick was an integral part of the Phils' NL title. Andy hit .288 with 24 home runs, both career highs.

5. The Phillies beat the Brooklyn Dodgers, 4-1, in dramatic fashion. Those Dodgers were managed by ex-Phils skipper Burt Shotton. After losing to the Phillies, Shotton was fired by the Dodgers.

6. Don Newcombe was the Dodger pitcher who started, and took the loss. Newcombe came into that game looking for his 20th win of the season.

7. That was the Dodgers' Cal Abrams. With the score tied at 1 in the bottom of the ninth, Abrams tried to score on a base hit to center by Duke Snider. Ashburn's throw nailed him by a mile, and wiped out the potential winning run. It's one of the most famous plays in Phillies history, and one that saved the club's second pennant. Abrams, by the way, was a Philadelphia native. And the Dodgers' third–base coach, Milt Stock, who waved Abrams home, was a third baseman on the 1915 Phillies. The '50 season finale was the last game Stock coached for the Dodgers. He was fired along with manager Burt Shotton.

8. Believe it or not, it was pitcher Robin Roberts. After pitching a full nine innings of one-run ball, Roberts led off the 10th with a single. He went to second on a base hit. Ashburn then tried to move him on a sacrifice, but Roberts was thrown out at third.

9. That was Dick Sisler in the 10th. Maybe the biggest and most famous home run in Phillies history. Certainly one of the most memorable. With the count one and two, Sisler crushed a fastball off Newcombe and sent it over the left-field fence at Ebbetts Field.

10. It was a three-run shot. Roberts' single got things going in the 10th. Eddie Waitkus followed with a single of his own. After the Dodgers cut down Roberts at third on Ashburn's sacrifice attempt, Sisler came to the plate with one out. The rest is Phillies history!

11. Robin Roberts pitched all 10 innings. After the Phils went ahead 4-1 in the top of the 10th, Roberts retired the Dodgers in order in the home half. In fact, both starting pitchers went the distance that day. The Dodgers' Don Newcombe also

pitched all 10. Roberts walked three, struck out two, and gave up only five hits. The only run he allowed came on a sixth–inning, solo homer by Pee Wee Reese.

12. The pennant-clinching victory over the Dodgers on the season's final day was Roberts' 20th of the year to lead the staff. It was the first 20-win season of his career. Roberts would win 20 or more in each of the next five seasons.

13. He saved 22. Konstanty appeared in a record 74 games that season, going 16-7, with a 2.66 ERA and the 22 saves. Many feel he was the chief reason the Phillies captured the NL flag.

14. That would be native Philadelphian Del Ennis. The Phillies outfielder blasted 31 homers and knocked in 126 runs in 1950. The 126 RBI led the league. With those kind of power numbers, Ennis finished fourth in the MVP voting.

15. Once again, it was Ennis. He took the Triple Crown among the Phillies that season. Ennis batted .311 to pace the Phils. Ashburn was second at .303. They were the only "Whiz Kids" to hit .300. And 1950 was a career year for Ennis. His .311 average and his RBI total of 126 were career highs, while his 31 homers tied his career best. After 1950, Ennis played nine more seasons in the majors, but never hit .300 again.

16. The speedster from Tilden, Nebraska, that's who. Richie Ashburn legged-out a league-high 14 triples in 1950. Richie hit 97 triples as a Phillie, fourth on the club's all-time list. During the '50 season, he also swiped 14 bases.

17. That catcher's name is Stan Lopata. He was the backup catcher for the 1950 Phils. In the pennant-clincher vs. the Dodgers, Lopata pinch-ran for Andy Seminick in the top of the ninth inning and remained in the game.

18. Andy Seminick was the igniter. Some bad blood developed between the Phillies and Giants during an August series, culminating with Seminick sliding hard into Giants second baseman Bill Rigney. The two went at it, prompting what Rich Westcott and Frank Bilovsky called in *The Phillies Encyclopedia*, "one of the rougher brawls in Shibe Park history." The team lived up to its nickname "The Fightin' Phils" that year, as earlier in the season they engaged in a bench-clearing melee with Cincinnati.

19. Dick Sisler, the hero of the win over Brooklyn. Sisler's father, George, played from 1915 to 1930, mostly with the St. Louis

Browns. The elder Sisler had over 2,800 hits and a career batting average of .340. Ironically, George was working as a scout for the Dodgers in 1950, and was watching from seats behind the Brooklyn dugout when Dick hit his famous HR.

20. Eddie Sawyer guided the "Whiz Kids" to the NL pennant in 1950. He had two separate tours of duty with the club: 1948 to 1952 and 1958 to 1960. His 390 wins rank fifth among Phillies managers.

▶ EXTRA BASE HIT

The relief pitcher extraordinaire of 1950, Jim Konstanty. "Big Jim" received 18 first–place votes to easily outdistance runner–up Stan Musial, who hit .346 for the Cardinals that year. Konstanty became the second Phillie ever to be voted the league's MVP.

6

1964

The mere thought of the 1964 season still sends shivers down the spines of the Phillies fans who lived through it. Is it an exaggeration to suggest that an entire fan base was left emotionally scarred and traumatized? The '64 Phillies were the best team in the National League for 150 games. Unfortunately, the season lasted 162. It was that last stretch that killed them. While they're remembered for a monumental September collapse, many of the players from that club are recalled fondly, and remain fan favorites to this day. Although for some fans, no doubt the scars still run deep, the healing powers of '80 and '08 not withstanding!

1. In 1964, what was the Phillies' lead in the NL with 12 games to play?
2. How many consecutive games did they lose in September?
3. What was the Phillies' largest lead in the standings during the '64 season?
4. How many days did the '64 Phillies spend in first place?
5. On September 21, 1964, which player stole home to give the Reds a 1-0 victory over the Phillies?
6. In what inning did that theft of home occur, and who was the Reds' slugger at bat?
7. How many shutout wins did the Phillies pitching staff earn in 1964?
8. What two future Phillies managers were members of the '64 team?

9. What two former Philadelphia Athletics played on the '64 Phils?
10. Who led the '64 Phillies in both HRs and RBI?

More Trivia from 1964

11. The 1964 Phillies won 92 games. How many did they win at home?
12. What happened in the game vs. the Mets on June 21st?
13. Who played catcher for the Phillies that day?
14. Which Phillies infielder led the National League in errors in 1964?
15. Who was the manager of the '64 Phillies? (Come on, that's an easy one!)
16. Who was the starting second baseman on the '64 Phillies?
17. How many HRs did Richie Allen hit in 1964?
18. Which ex-Phillies hurler handed the club its 10th straight loss in September 1964?
19. The Phillies were "no-hit" during the '64 season. By whom were they held hitless, and on what date?
20. Who had the highest batting average on the '64 Phillies?

▶ **EXTRA BASE HIT**

Which player referred to the '64 season as "The Year of the Blue Snow"?

ANSWERS

1. The Phillies had a $6^1/_2$–game lead with a dozen to go, and a magic number of seven.
2. They lost 10. The roof caved in as the Phillies lost every game from September 21st to September 30th.
3. The Phils' largest lead of the '64 season was $7^1/_2$ games on August 20th. And then came September!
4. The '64 Phillies spent 112 days in first place, including a stretch from July 16th to September 26th. On September 27th,

they lost to the Braves, 14-8, to fall one game back, and they never regained the lead.

5. That was Chico Ruiz, who lives forever in Phillies infamy. Ruiz was a 25–year–old rookie infielder from Santo Domingo, Cuba, who stole just 11 bases that season. But his plate pilfer that night started the Phillies on their downward spiral. The 1-0 loss was the first of their 10 consecutive losses.

6. It was in the sixth inning. Frank Robinson was at the plate with two out. Art Mahaffey was on the mound. Following Ruiz's steal, Mahaffey got Robinson to ground out, but the damage was done. From there, the only offense the Phils could muster was a pair of doubles by Wes Covington, and both times they failed to get the run home.

7. There were 17 shutout wins in '64. That was the second most in the NL. Every starter tossed at least one. Bunning led the way with five.

8. They were Dallas Green and Pat Corrales. Green, who, of course, managed the '80 Phillies to the World Series title, was a 29–year–old relief pitcher. He appeared in 26 games, going 2-1 with a 5.79 ERA. Corrales was called up to the majors in '54 and played in two games. In his only at–bat, he walked and scored a run. Corrales replaced Green as Phillies skipper. He managed the club in 1982 and part of '83.

9. They were Vic Power and Bobby Shantz. Power, a .284 lifetime hitter, was acquired from California to play first base after Frank Thomas went down with a thumb injury. Power was 36 at the time, and had little "power" left. In 18 games, he batted only .208, with no homers and just three RBI. Shantz was 38 and in his final season. The three-time All-Star and former American League MVP appeared in 14 games after joining the team in August. He won one and lost one, and had a 2.25 ERA in 32 innings of work.

10. Johnny Callison led with 31 HRs and 104 RBI. The year 1964 was perhaps the best of his 16 seasons in the majors. His RBI total was a career high. He was third in the league in homers, and was the runner-up in the MVP balloting.

11. They won exactly half at home. The team went 46-35 at Connie Mack Stadium and 46-35 on the road.

12. If you know that Father's Day fell on June 21st that year, then you probably know that was the day that Jim Bunning

pitched a perfect game against the Mets. Bunning, a father of seven, turned in the greatest performance of his Hall of Fame career. Bunning struck out 10, in retiring 27 Mets in a row. It was the second no-hitter of Bunning's career, and the first regular season perfect game in 42 years. It was also the first perfect game in National League history. The perfect game earned Bunning an appearance on *The Ed Sullivan Show* later that night.

13. It was Gus Triandos. He platooned with Clay Dalrymple during the '64 season, and was behind the plate for Bunning's perfect game. Triandos went two for four with a double and two RBI that day. Interestingly, he came to the Phillies from the Tigers in the same off-season trade that also brought Bunning to town.

14. It was the rookie third baseman, Richie Allen, who made 41 errors that season. Allen was a converted outfielder who was playing third for the first time in his career. The way he swung the bat that year, the Phillies could live with his error-prone defense.

15. The "Little General," Gene Mauch. Although he never won a championship, you can make the case that Mauch is the greatest manager in franchise history. No one possessed a higher baseball IQ. But Mauch is better remembered for not winning "the big one." The year 1964 is exhibit A. In addition, his California Angels teams twice blew a lead of two games to one in the American League Championship Series. In 1986, he was one strike away from his first trip to the World Series, only to lose the ALCS in heartbreaking fashion.

16. The ever-popular Tony Taylor. Always a fan favorite in his 15 years as a Phillie, Taylor batted .251 in 154 games that ill-fated season.

17. Allen smashed 29 HRs that season, second on the team, and to that point, most by a rookie in franchise history. He also led the league in runs, total bases, and tied for the league lead with 13 triples.

18. That would be Curt Simmons. Simmons was one of the young stars of the "Whiz Kids" and a three–time All–Star as a Phillie. But the Phillies thought he was done in 1960 and released him. St. Louis signed him and Curt pitched for the

Cardinals until 1966. In '64, he went 18-9, including an 8-5 win over the Phillies on September 30th, which helped dash the Phils' pennant hopes. Instead, Simmons went on to pitch for the Cardinals in the World Series that year.

19. Hall of Famer Sandy Koufax pitched a no-hitter against the Phillies on June 4, 1964. (That's right, 6/4/64!) The reigning MVP and Cy Young Award winner, Koufax struck out 12 Phillies that night. It would've been a perfect game, if not for a fourth–inning walk to Richie Allen. It was Koufax's sixth win in what would be a 19–win season for the left–handed great. It was also the third of his four career no-hitters.

20. Allen batted .318 to lead the '64 Phillies. It was also the fifth highest average in the league that season. Add his 29 HRs and 91 RBI, and it's easy to see why he was voted the National League Rookie of the Year. Allen was only the second Phillie ever to be so honored.

► EXTRA BASE HIT

The man who caught Bunning's perfect game, Gus Triandos, called it "The Year of the Blue Snow."

7

1980

Tuesday, October 21, 1980. The Philadelphia Police K-9 Corps, with their attack dogs in tow, ring the Veterans Stadium field. Their presence adds a militaristic feel to the moment. It also screams to the 65,000 in attendance: "If you're planning on getting out of hand, guess again."

There are two outs and two strikes. The home team leads by three, but the bases are loaded, and the potential go-ahead run is at bat.

On the mound, an exhausted pitcher summons every ounce of energy he has left. He rears back and fires a fastball that leaves his hand and darts to the plate. The batter swings and misses. Strike three. Ballgame over. Pandemonium ensues.

It's 11:29 p.m. in South Philadelphia, and after 97 years, the Phillies have won the World Series for the first time. For the team's long-suffering fans, it's a moment that stands still in time forever.

But getting to that moment wasn't easy. The '80 season took many twists and turns, wound through many highs and lows, before ending in a parade down Broad Street. This section is devoted to the first Phillies season to result in a championship.

1. Which player had the highest batting average on the 1980 Phillies (minimum of 500 at-bats)?
2. Who led the 1980 Phillies in stolen bases?

3. Which rookie pitcher, called up in September, played a pivotal role in the stretch drive in 1980, and how many games did he win?
4. Whose clubhouse tirade in September 1980 sparked the team in the pennant race?
5. What team did the '80 Phillies beat on the final weekend of the regular season to win the NL East?
6. Whose game-winning home run clinched the division title for the Phils in 1980?
7. How many HRs did Mike Schmidt hit in 1980?
8. Who was the winning pitcher in the division clincher?
9. How many games did the Phillies win in the 1980 regular season?
10. What was the Phillies' winningest month during the 1980 regular season?

More from 1980

11. Which Phillie played in the most games in 1980?
12. Which member of the '80 Phillies was a former pro basketball player?
13. How many games did Steve Carlton win in 1980?
14. What former American League Cy Young Award–winner pitched in 10 games for the Phillies in 1980?
15. Which starting pitcher led the '80 Phils in losses?
16. Which member of the '80 Phillies was the son of a major leaguer and the father of two future major leaguers?
17. Who was the third–base coach for the '80 Phillies?
18. Who was the pitching coach for the '80 Phillies?
19. Who was the backup catcher on the '80 Phils?
20. Which starting pitcher was lost for the season in May due to injury?
21. Which member of the '80 Phillies was also a member of the broadcast team and would do postgame interviews in uniform?
22. Which three players represented the Phillies in the 1980 All-Star Game?

23. How many players named "Vukovich" were members of the '80 Phillies?
24. Who led the '80 team in pinch hits?
25. Who had the highest batting average among the starting infielders?

▶ EXTRA BASE HIT

What college did Bake McBride attend?

1. Right–fielder Bake McBride hit .309 that year, the highest average on the team.
2. Lonnie Smith stole 33 bases, the most on the '80 Phils. Smith was caught stealing 13 times, also most among the '80 Phils. It was his rookie season and in 100 games, the speedy outfielder batted .339 in 298 at-bats and finished third in the Rookie of the Year voting.
3. That, of course, is Marty Bystrom. Only 21 years old, Bystrom made five starts and won them all. He made his major league debut on September 7th, tossing a perfect inning in relief vs. the Dodgers. Three days later, he made his first career start, and went all the way on a five-hit shutout of the Mets. Bystrom was 5-0 with a 1.50 ERA that final month of the season. The Phillies don't win the pennant without his contribution. Bystrom seemed headed for stardom, but he won just 24 games the rest of his career, and five years later, he was out of baseball.
4. It was General Manager Paul Owens. On September 1st, before a game in San Francisco, Owens threw an angry tirade that was totally out of character. Owens, then 56, actually challenged each player to a fight. Dallas Green famously went ballistic between games of a doubleheader in Pittsburgh, but that was in August. Owens' outburst really got their attention. The Phillies went 19-10 the rest of the way.
5. The Montreal Expos, with whom the Phillies were tied atop the standings heading into a three-game series in Montreal.
6. It was Mike Schmidt in game two of the three-game series. The Phillies had taken the opener to give them a one-game

lead over the Expos. Naturally, a Phillies loss would set the stage for a decisive season finale. Schmidt wasn't about to let that happen. The game went extra innings, and in the top of the 11th, Schmidty crushed a two-run homer to break a 4-4 tie.

7. Schmidt hit 48. At the time, 48 was a new franchise, single-season record. The game-winner in Montreal was the last, and the biggest, giving the Phils the NL flag.

8. Tug McGraw, who retired the side in order in the bottom of the 11th. McGraw pitched the final three innings that day, retiring nine of the 10 batters he faced.

9. That would be 91. They finished 91-71 (losing a meaningless season finale in extra innings). The World Champs won 49 at home and 42 on the road. They were 32-28 in one–run games that season. Their longest winning streak was six. Their longest losing streak was six.

10. It was September: 19-10, including eight of the last 11, Bystrom winning three in that stretch. But the season actually ended October 5th, and the four straight they won, from October 1st to 4th, was the biggest of the year.

11. Pete Rose played in all 162 that season.

12. It was relief pitcher Ron Reed. After a standout collegiate career at Notre Dame, Reed was drafted third overall by the Detroit Pistons in the 1965 NBA Draft. Reed played two seasons for the Pistons, averaging eight points and six and a half rebounds per game.

13. Lefty won 24, the most in the NL that year, and the second-most of his career. Carlton went 24-9, with a 2.34 ERA to win his second career Cy Young Award. His 304 innings pitched were also the most among NL hurlers.

14. That would be Sparky Lyle. He was acquired from Texas in September 1980 for a player to be named later (Kevin Saucier). Lyle gave up three earned runs in 14 innings, notching two saves. Lyle won the 1977 Cy Young Award while with the Yankees.

15. Randy Lerch was the pitcher. Individually, it wasn't a banner year for the six–foot, five–inch left–hander. He went 4-14 with a 5.16 ERA. Lerch was traded to Milwaukee the following March.

16. That's an easy one: catcher Bob Boone. The son of Ray Boone, an infielder for six different teams from 1948 to 1960. The father of Bret, who played 14 seasons from 1992 to 2005, and Aaron, who came up in 1997 and played with Washington in 2008. Bret was a three-time All-Star. Aaron is best remembered for his walk-off HR that won the 2003 AL pennant for the Yankees.

17. That was Lee Elia. The graduate of Olney High in Philadelphia spent two seasons as a Phillies coach. A few years later, he returned to manage the club.

18. Herm Starrette was the pitching coach for the '80 Phillies.

19. Keith Moreland was the backup catcher. Moreland hit .314 in 62 games.

20. Larry Christenson made just 14 starts before elbow surgery in late May ended his season. At the time, Christenson was 5-1, with a 4.01 ERA. Bob Walk was called up to replace him. Walk played a key role, going 11-7.

21. Tim McCarver, who was already in the broadcast booth when he was signed as a free agent on September 1st. That allowed him to become one of the few big leaguers whose careers spanned four decades. (He came up with St. Louis in 1959.) McCarver appeared in six games for the Phillies in 1980, going 1-5 with a walk, and two RBI. He spent three years as a Phillies broadcaster before joining the Mets. McCarver later became a game analyst on network television.

22. The three were Carlton, Rose, and Schmidt. Carlton, who was the starting pitcher the previous year, did not play. Neither did Schmidt. Rose had one at-bat. He grounded into an inning-ending double play in the sixth. The NL won the game, 4-2.

23. In 1980, the Phils led the league in Vukovichs. There was John Vukovich, reserve third baseman, and there was George Vukovich, who was a reserve outfielder. The two "Vukes" were not related. John appeared in 49 games. George played in 78, in what was his rookie year. His career ended following the '85 season. John played parts of 10 seasons in the big leagues, and was later a longtime Phillies coach.

24. Del Unser with 12. It was the only time in the three-plus seasons that they were teammates that Unser had more pinch

hits than Greg Gross, the Phillies' all-time leader in the category.

25. If you said Rose, you are wrong. No, not Schmidty. And it's not Bowa, so it must be…Manny Trillo. The second baseman hit .292, 10 points higher than Rose. Schmidt had a .286 batting average, but did win league MVP honors.

▶ EXTRA BASE HIT

Bake McBride attended Westminster College in his hometown of Fulton, Missouri. Westminster College is where Winston Churchill made his famous "Iron Curtain" speech in 1946. It was also at Westminster College where Soviet premier Mikhail Gorbachev announced the end of the Cold War in 1992.

8

1983

Three seasons after winning their first World Series title, the Phillies were back in the Fall Classic. The "Pope," Paul Owens, came down from the front office to cajole a group of veterans, including a collection of future Hall of Famers, to the franchise's fourth NL pennant.

The '83 Phillies are somewhat overlooked in the annals of Phils history. Maybe because they were an older bunch. Maybe because they didn't win it all like the guys in 1980. Maybe because at their core was a group of former Cincinnati Reds.

They weren't as beloved as the "Whiz Kids" of '50, or the "worst to first" '93 Phillies. Their offensive statistics weren't overly impressive. Only two players hit .300. Only one drove in 100 runs. But they won 90 games and rose to the occasion late in the season like few Phillies teams ever have.

In this section, we test your knowledge of the 1983 Phillies, one of only six teams in franchise history to play for a World Championship.

1. Can you name the two Phillies who batted .300 in 1983 (minimum 200 at-bats)?
2. What was the average age of the players on the '83 Phillies?
3. Who was the oldest player on the '83 Phillies?
4. Who started the season as the club's manager?
5. In what place in the standings were the '83 Phillies when Paul Owens took over as manager?

6. Who was the only '83 Phillie to score 100 runs?
7. Who was the only starting pitcher on the '83 Phillies who had a better than .500 record?
8. Can you name the former Rookies of the Year who were members of the '83 Phils?
9. Can you name the future Hall of Famers who were members of the '83 Phils?
10. Which pitcher on the '83 Phillies won the Cy Young Award the following season?
11. Name the closer who led the '83 Phillies with 25 saves.
12. What team did Steve Carlton beat in 1983 to earn his 300th career victory?
13. What was the '83 Phillies' longest winning streak?
14. In what ballpark did the '83 Phillies clinch the NL East?
15. Who was the starting shortstop on the '83 Phillies?

▶ EXTRA BASE HIT

What was the nickname of the '83 Phillies?

1. They were Joe Lefebvre and Greg Gross. Lefebvre hit .310 in 258 at-bats. Gross, .302 in 245. That was it. Unless you count Darren Daulton, who went 1–for–3 in two games. Technically, Gary Matthews led the team in batting that year. He hit .258 in 446 at-bats, highest among the regulars with at least 400 at-bats.

2. The average was 32 years old.

3. At 42 years old, Pete Rose was the oldest player on the team that season. Despite his advanced age and without the aid of performance–enhancing drugs, Pete played in 151 games. That was just seven fewer than team leader Ivan DeJesus. Pete batted .245 for the Phils in '83.

4. Pat Corrales managed the club for the first 85 games, then was fired and replaced by Paul Owens. Once upon a time, Owens managed Corrales in the minor leagues. But now he was firing him, and succeeding him. Corrales landed on his feet two weeks later when he was hired by the Cleveland

Indians. He is one of the few men to manage a team in both leagues in the same season.

5. Ironically, the Phillies were in first place. Firing a first-place manager is very rare, but Owens thought the team was underachieving. In fact, they were only one game over .500 at 43-42.

6. It was Mike Schmidt, who scored 104 runs. Next closest on the list was Joe Morgan with 72. Schmidt was also the only player on the team to drive in 100, finishing with 109 RBI on the season. In addition, he clouted 40 home runs. It was the third and final time in his career that he hit 40 or more homers.

7. It was John Denny, who went 19-6. Actually, 1983 was a career year for the right–hander who, prior to that season, had never won more than 14 games, and who would not win more than 11 in a season again. Denny won the Cy Young in a landslide, becoming the first Phillie not named Steve Carlton to earn the award.

8. There were two of them: Pete Rose, who won it in 1963, and Gary Matthews, who won it 10 years later.

9. There were four of them: Joe Morgan was inducted in 1990; Steve Carlton in 1994; Mike Schmidt was enshrined the following year; and Tony Perez made it to Cooperstown in 2000.

10. It was relief pitcher Willie Hernandez. He joined the Phillies in May '83, via a trade with the Cubs, and went 9-4 with seven saves. In the World Series, he didn't allow a run in three appearances. But the following March, he was shipped to Detroit and that's when his career took off. Hernandez had 32 saves and a 1.92 ERA to walk away with Cy Young honors and help the '84 Tigers win the World Series. In his first three years in Detroit, Hernandez saved 87 games and was named to the AL All-Star team each season.

11. His name is Al Holland. Nicknamed "Mr. T," the bearded Holland took over for the veteran Tug McGraw as the go-to lefty out of the pen. Holland's best year was 1983. He appeared in 68 games, saving 25 and winning eight. His ERA was 2.25. He had 100 strikeouts in 92 innings, and he walked only 30 batters all season. "Mr. T" was key in '83!

12. Ironically, it was his former team, the St. Louis Cardinals. On September 23, 1983, Carlton beat the redbirds 6-2 in St. Louis for his 300th career victory. He struck out 12 in eight innings, and even knocked in a run to help his cause. That night Carlton became baseball's 16th 300-game winner.

13. It was 11 in a row. Carlton's 300th was number eight in that streak. It spanned from September 16th to the 26th, and it cemented the division crown. Talk about coming up big when it counts; not only did they win 11 in a row, but 14 of their last 16 games.

14. The Phillies celebrated in the friendly confines of Wrigley Field in Chicago, site of many a big victory for the Phils over the years. This one, on September 28th, was a 13-6 final with former Cub Willie Hernandez earning the win. Catcher Bo Diaz had five hits, including two home runs. Schmidty hit his 40th of the season, and also tripled. Ex-Phillie Dick Ruthven was the losing pitcher.

15. None other than Ivan DeJesus, who replaced Larry Bowa in the Phillies infield the previous season. In '83, DeJesus batted .254, and had a fielding percentage of .966.

► EXTRA BASE HIT

They were called the "Wheeze Kids." It was in reference to the advanced average age of the club, and with a play on the nickname of the popular Phillies team of 33 years earlier. "Wheeze Kids" . . . how great is that?

9

1993

The Phillies were the hottest story in town during the summer of 1993. Fans packed the Vet each and every night, as attendance for the season topped 3.1 million. The '93 Phils were a motley but memorable crew. "Gypsies, tramps, and thieves," Darren Daulton called them. Led by "Dutch," "Nails," "Krukker," and the "Wild Thing," the '93 Phils were a mix of grizzled vets and youthful talents who took the National League by storm and surprise. Blazing out of the gate in April, the '93 Phillies never looked back and roared from last place the previous season to first place in the NL East, and ultimately all the way to the World Series! Unfortunately for Phillies fans, that team did everything except win it all.

It was an unforgettable season, thanks to some unforgettable characters and some unforgettable baseball. How much do you remember about the 1993 Phillies?

1. Who was the Opening Day starting pitcher for the Phillies in 1993?
2. Who was the Phillies' Opening Day shortstop in '93?
3. Who was the number–five starter in the Phillies' pitching rotation in '93?
4. Who had the highest batting average among the '93 Phillies (minimum 400 at-bats)?
5. Name the only player on the '93 Phillies who drove in 100 runs.

6. What was the '93 team's largest lead in the standings?
7. Which member of the coaching staff was a former World Series MVP?
8. Who was the '93 Phillies' oldest player?
9. Who was the highest-paid player on the '93 Phillies?
10. Two players shared the lead in HRs on the '93 Phillies. Can you name them?

More About 1993

11. Which '93 Phillie delivered the game-winning hit in the latest-ending game in major league history? And off whom did he get that hit?
12. Which member of the '93 Phillies didn't spend a single day in the minor leagues?
13. Who was the '93 Phillie who suffered from Tourette's syndrome?
14. Name the only member of the '93 Phillies who held one of baseball's major single-season records.
15. Which two members of the '93 Phils finally won World Series rings with the '97 Florida Marlins?
16. Name the Phillie who in 1993 led the National League in at-bats, hits, walks, and runs.
17. Which member of the '93 Phillies later became the club's hitting coach?
18. Which member of the '93 Phillies was the only position player drafted by the Phils in the first round?
19. Can you name the Temple University alum who was a member of the '93 Phillies?
20. How many games did Mitch Williams save in 1993?
21. What two pitchers tied for the team lead in victories in 1993?
22. Who batted cleanup for the '93 Phils?
23. What was "Macho Row"?
24. Which members of the '93 Phillies also played for the '83 Phillies? (There were two.)
25. For how many games were the Phillies in first place during the '93 season?

▶ **EXTRA BASE HIT**

Which players on the '93 Phillies represented the team in the All-Star Game?

1. Terry Mulholland, who went 12-9, with a 3.25 ERA in '93. On Opening Day, Mulholland beat the Astros in Houston 3-1, going the distance on a four-hitter. The Phillies were off and running.

2. Juan Bell started at shortstop that day. It wasn't a day he'd like to remember. Bell went 0–for–4 and made two errors. He batted .200 in 24 games, and was placed on waivers by the end of May.

3. It was Ben Riviera. His line that season: 13-9, 5.02 ERA. Curt Schilling, Danny Jackson, Tommy Greene, Mulholland, and Riviera. It was as deep a rotation as the Phils have ever had. Each guy won at least a dozen games.

4. John Kruk, with a .316 average. One thing about Krukker, he could always hit. Kruk had a great year in '93. He had an on-base percentage of .430. He walked 111 times, scored 100 runs, and knocked in 85. He might've been overweight, he might've needed a haircut and a shave, his uniform may have been a disheveled mess, but boy could he hit. And Kruk personified the spirit of the '93 Phillies.

5. That would be the team's unquestioned leader, Darren Daulton. "Dutch" drove in 105 runs that year, his second consecutive season with 100 or more.

6. It was 11^1/$_2$ games after a 5-3 win over the Mets on June 13th. That was their largest margin of the season. They'd win the division by three, after clinching with five games to play.

7. Pitching coach Johnny Podres was the first-ever World Series MVP, winning the inaugural award in 1955. As a young pitcher for the Brooklyn Dodgers, Podres won two games in the '55 Series vs. the Yankees, including a shutout in the decisive Game 7.

8. At age 40, relief pitcher Larry Andersen. The current Phillies radio analyst was in his 18th season in the bigs, and starting his second tour with the Phils.

9. Baseball-reference.com lists the highest-paid '93 Phillie as closer Mitch Williams, who earned a salary of about 3.5 million dollars.

10. Darren Daulton and Pete Incaviglia both slugged a team-leading 24 HRs.

11. It was Mitch Williams. In his only at-bat of the year, Williams' single drove in the game-winning run to end the second game of the rain-delayed doubleheader with San Diego. Mitch's walk-off hit came at 4:40 a.m. He hit it off Trevor Hoffman, who would one day become baseball's all-time saves leader!

12. Outfielder Pete Incaviglia went straight from Oklahoma State to the big leagues.

13. Outfielder Jim Eisenreich suffered from Tourette's. He was out of baseball from 1984 to 1987 while undergoing treatment. Eisenreich now runs a charitable foundation that benefits children with the disorder.

14. That was reliever Bobby Thigpen. As the White Sox closer in 1990, Thigpen set a major league record with 57 saves. Thigpen's record stood until 2008, when the Angels' Francisco Rodriquez notched 62 saves. In 1993, he was acquired by the Phils in an August trade with the White Sox. Thigpen pitched in 17 games for the Phillies, going 3-1 with a 6.05 ERA. In the '93 World Series, he pitched $2^2/_3$ scoreless innings. He signed with Seattle as a free agent the following off-season. But by the end of April 1994, he was out of baseball.

15. The two were Darren Daulton and Jim Eisenreich. Four years later, they achieved with Florida what they could not with the Phillies, as the Marlins beat Cleveland to win the World Series.

16. That would be Lenny Dykstra. "Nails" had a monster year in '93: 637 at–bats and 194 hits. He walked 129 times and scored 143 runs. Dykstra had an on-base percentage of .420. His batting average that year was .305, and he also added 19 home runs.

17. That would be Milt Thompson. He has worked with Phillies hitters since 2005. Prior to that, he was the club's first base coach. In '93, Thompson hit .262 in 129 games, and had a huge postseason, batting .313 in the World Series. He played over 11 seasons in the big leagues and had a career batting average of .274.

18. Reserve first baseman Ricky Jordan was drafted 22nd overall in 1983. He was the only position player on the team drafted by the Phillies in the first round.

19. His name is Jeff Manto. The third baseman from Bristol, Pennsylvania appeared in eight games that season, going 1–for–18 at the plate. But in 1995, Manto hit 17 home runs in 89 games for the Orioles; four of those HRs came in four consecutive at-bats. Manto played college ball at Temple in the mid-1980s. He later went on to manage the Phils' single-A club at Lakewood.

20. Williams had 43 saves in 1993 to set what was then a new club record.

21. Curt Schilling and Tommy Greene each won 16 games that season to lead all Phillies pitchers.

22. It was Dave Hollins. The third baseman batted fourth in the lineup in 143 games.

23. "Macho Row" referred to the corner of the clubhouse where Daulton, Kruk, Dykstra, Incaviglia, Hollins, and Williams kept their lockers.

24. They were Larry Andersen and Darren Daulton. L.A. was a relief pitcher on both pennant winners. In '83, he appeared in 17 games and had an ERA of 2.39. At age 30, he was one of the younger "Wheez Kids." Daulton was a September callup in '83. He played in two games, going 1–for–3 at the plate.

25. The total is 161. The only time the '93 Phils were out of first was April 9th, following a loss to the Cubs, which dropped them a half-game back. They were in first on May 1st, June 1st, July 1st, August 1st and September 1st. They're the only team in club history that can say that.

▶ **EXTRA BASE HIT**

The Phillies sent four players to the All-Star Game that was played in Baltimore that year. Daulton, Kruk, Hollins, and Mulholland were named to the NL squad. Daulton and Kruk were voted as starters. Mulholland was tabbed as the game's starting pitcher. He worked the first two innings, giving up one run on a solo homer by game MVP Kirby Puckett. Daulton and Kruk both went 0-3. Kruk whiffed twice. (Remember him facing Randy Johnson?) Hollins doubled in his only at-bat as the NL went down, 9-3.

10

20-oh-Great!

To borrow a famous line: It was the best of times, it was the worst of times. In 2008, we were faced with a faltering economy. The credit crunch and mortgage crisis sent banks reeling. Homes were being foreclosed upon, jobs were being lost. The government was forced to bail out Wall Street. The stock market fluctuated wildly by hundreds of points each day. In addition, we were in the midst of a heated and contentious presidential campaign, and the wars in Iraq and Afghanistan raged on.

Through it all, Phillies fans turned their lonely eyes to Uncle Chuck Manuel's boys, and unlike so many of their predecessors, Uncle Chuck's boys didn't disappoint. In 2008, the hometown team provided the perfect escape. After a loss to the Marlins on September 10th, the Phillies were $3^1/_2$ games back in the NL East. All they did was win 12 of their next 15 to clinch the division. The 2008 Phils won 24 of their last 30, with an 11–and–3 record in the postseason. That's how you win championships. And that's what the 2008 Phillies did: four games to one over the Tampa Bay Rays in a wild, wet, wonderful World Series. A team built for the long ball with Utley, Howard, and Burrell got great pitching. Quality starts from Hamels, Myers, Moyer, and Blanton helped deliver a long-awaited parade down Broad Street. They did it. They ended the Phillies' 28-year championship drought. They actually did it.

Relive the best of Phillies times in the following questions.

1. What was the highest total of runs the 2008 Phillies scored in a single game during the regular season?
2. Who had the highest batting average on the 2008 Phillies (minimum 300 at-bats)?
3. Which hitter led the 2008 Phillies in walks?
4. What is manager Charlie Manuel's middle name?
5. Which member of the 2008 Phillies made it to the big leagues for the first time at age 33?
6. Who led the 2008 Phillies in hits?
7. Name the longest-tenured Phillie on the 2008 team.
8. Which member of the 2008 Phillies led the league in home runs off left-handed pitchers?
9. Which pitcher led the 2008 Phillies in victories?
10. Which member of the 2008 Phillies was born in Canada?

More from 20-oh-Great

11. Who was the only 2008 Phillie to play in every game in 2008?
12. Which pitcher was sent to the minors after having been the Opening Day starter?
13. Which 2008 Phillie was benched twice during the regular season: first for not running out a pop-up, and again for showing up late to a game?
14. Which member of the 2008 Phillies graduated from the same high school as Hall of Fame great Frank Robinson?
15. Which former Phillie sent an e-mail of encouragement to the team prior to a crucial series with the Mets?
16. Which starting pitcher joined the team in a July trade?
17. How many games did closer Brad Lidge save in 2008?
18. What was the Phillies record in 2008, when leading after eight innings?
19. Who was the third–base coach for the 2008 Phillies?
20. Which member of the 2008 Phillies was born in Eureka Springs, Arkansas?

Still More from '08

21. What was the Phillies payroll on Opening Day 2008?
22. Which member of the 2008 Phillies had a stepfather, grandfather, and uncle who all played in the major leagues?
23. What do the initials J.C. stand for in pitcher J.C. Romero's name?
24. What do the initials J.A. stand for in pitcher J.A. Happ's name?
25. Which member of the 2008 Phillies was the NL's leading vote-getter in the '08 All-Star Game?
26. Which member of the 2008 Phillies coaching staff was the leading vote-getter in the '80 All-Star Game?
27. Which member of the 2008 Phillies coaching staff, while as a player, got his first major league hit off Hall of Famer Juan Marichal?
28. What song is played at the ballpark when Chase Utley comes to the plate?
29. To what team did closer Brad Lidge suffer his only loss of 2008?
30. How did the Phillies secure the final out of the division-clinching win over Washington?

▶ **EXTRA BASE HIT**

Entering the World Series, who was the only member of the 2008 Phillies with a World Series ring?

ANSWERS

1. The 2008 Phillies scored 20 runs in a game twice. On May 26th at home vs. Colorado, the Phils banged out 19 hits and won it 20-5. On June 13th in St. Louis, they scored 20 runs on 21 hits to beat the Cardinals, 20-2.

2. It was Shane Victorino. The center fielder hit .293 in 570 at-bats. Shane finished one point better than Chase Utley, who hit .292 in 607 at-bats. Greg Dobbs hit .301, but in only 226 at-bats.

3. Pat Burrell drew 102 bases on balls, the most on the team in 2008. He was the only player on the team to top 100 walks.
4. It's Fuqua, as in Charles Fuqua Manuel Jr.
5. That would be Chris Coste. The backup catcher first made it to the majors with the Phillies in May 2006 at age 33. His autobiography, published in 2008, is titled *The 33–year–old Rookie.*
6. Chase Utley, who rapped out 177 hits in 2008. Shane Victorino led the team in singles with 115.
7. That's the left fielder, Pat Burrell; 2008 marked Burrell's ninth full season with the Phillies. He made his debut on May 24, 2000. Jimmy Rollins came up in September 2000.
8. Outfielder Jayson Werth, who bats right, hit 16 of his 24 home runs off lefties.
9. The ageless wonder, Jamie Moyer. The 45–year–old Moyer went 16-7 to lead the 2008 staff. He also had the fewest losses of any of the Phillies pitchers who made 19 or more starts in 2008.
10. Matt Stairs was born in St. John, New Brunswick in 1968.
11. First baseman Ryan Howard played in every game in 2008.
12. Brett Myers was the Opening Day starter in 2008, but struggled mightily through the first couple of months of the season. So the Phillies sent him down to the minors to regain his form and his confidence. It worked. Myers was like a new man when he was recalled. In August and September, he was one of the top pitchers in the National League, and a big reason why the Phillies advanced to win the World Series.
13. Jimmy Rollins, of all people, who was the reigning National League MVP. You'd think he, as one of the team's veteran leaders, would know better. But J-Roll was benched twice during the regular season for those transgressions. Charlie Manuel has only two rules for his players: hustle and be on time. And Rollins violated both. But Manuel, to his credit, sent a firm message to his club that no one, not even the reigning league MVP, is above the rest of the team. To Jimmy's credit, he accepted the punishment.
14. Relief pitcher Clay Condrey is a 1994 graduate of Navasota High School in Navasota, Texas. In addition to the great Frank Robinson, the school produced former big leaguer Gus Zernial.

15. The e–mailer was Mike Schmidt.
16. Right-handed starter Joe Blanton was acquired from the Oakland A's in exchange for three Phillies minor leaguers on July 17th. Blanton made 13 starts for the Phillies during the 2008 regular season, going 4-0, with a 4.20 ERA. He went 2-0 in three postseason starts.
17. Lidge lived up to his nickname "Lights Out," posting 41 saves in 2008. Those 41 represented every save opportunity he faced. Amazingly, Lidge was a perfect 41–for–41. Then he saved seven more in the postseason: 48–for–48 in 2008! Don't kid yourself—while Hamels, Howard, and Utley were all great, Lidge was the primary reason the Phillies won it all.
18. It was 79 and 0. When they led after eight, they didn't lose. Not once all season. Credit Lidge.
19. His name is Steve Smith.
20. Pat Burrell is the Arkansan. While he grew up in San Jose, California, and went to college in Miami, Burrell was born in Eureka Springs, Arkansas on October 10, 1976.
21. A franchise record $104,567,500.
22. That's Jayson Werth. His stepfather, Dennis Werth, played three seasons with the Yankees in the early '80s. His grandfather, Ducky Schofield, spent 19 years in the big leagues, winning the World Series with the '60 Pirates. Werth's uncle, Dick Schofield, had a 14-year big league career.
23. J.C. for Juan Carlos.
24. J.A. for James Anthony.
25. Chase Utley led all NL stars with 3,889,602 votes.
26. First–base coach Davey Lopes, the Dodgers' second baseman and a four–time All–Star, led all vote–getters for the 1980 game played at Dodger Stadium.
27. Bench coach Jimy Williams played in 14 games in the majors, got three hits in 13 at-bats, but the first one came off Marichal. Jimy also faced Hall of Famer Sandy Koufax in his first big league at-bat. Koufax struck him out.
28. Utley's song is Led Zeppelin's "Kashmir."
29. You're saying to yourself, "Wait a minute; Lidge went 2-0 with the 41 saves and a 1.95 ERA in '08; he didn't lose to anyone." And you'd be right, technically. But Lidge did have one blemish on his record in 2008. He was the losing pitcher in the All-Star Game. The answer is...the American League

All-Stars were the only team to beat Lidge in 2008. The Phils' closer pitched the 15th inning for the NL Stars. He gave up two singles and walked a batter to load the bases. Then the Rangers' Michael Young lifted a sacrifice fly that scored Justin Morneau of the Twins to give the AL a 4-3 win. Ironically, that loss would cost the Phillies home-field advantage in the World Series. Not that it mattered. In fact, it turned out to be a blessing in disguise for the Phillies, because it allowed them to clinch the Series at home.

30. On a dazzling double play with the bases loaded in the ninth, and the Phillies clinging to a one-run lead. The DP was started on a diving stop by Jimmy Rollins: Rollins to Utley to Howard, 6-4-3, and the Phillies had their second straight NL East title. It was just the beginning.

▶ EXTRA BASE HIT

That was reserve outfielder So Taguchi, who played for the 2006 World Series Champion St. Louis Cardinals.

11

Schmidt Happens

"Twenty years ago," said Mike Schmidt in announcing his retirement, "I left Dayton, Ohio with two very bad knees and the dream of playing major league baseball," his voice then trailing off into sobs. It was 1989, and with that the greatest career in Phillies history came to an end.

Is there any doubt that Schmidt is the greatest Phillie of all time? No one hit more home runs, drove in more runs, played in more games, had more at-bats, or more hits. No Phillie was a better all-around player than number 20, whose defense was as formidable as his slugging prowess. There isn't a Phillie who won more Gold Gloves. Forget Phillies history—Schmidty is arguably the greatest third baseman the game has ever seen. This section is where the Schmidt hits the fan!

1. Who wore uniform number 20 before Schmidt?
2. Where was Schmidt drafted in the 1971 Draft?
3. Whom did the Phillies take with their number–one pick in 1971?
4. What Hall of Famer was drafted just ahead of Schmidt in '71?
5. Who was the Phillies scout that signed Schmidt?
6. What college did Schmidt attend?
7. What did Schmidt study in college?
8. Against what team did Schmidt hit his first home run as a Phillie?
9. Off what pitcher did Mike hit his first home run?

10. Who was the Hall of Famer who was Mike's first professional manager?

More Schmidty

11. What was Mike's final career hit?
12. What did Mike do in his final career at-bat?
13. What was Mike's batting average in his first full season in the majors?
14. What was Mike's career batting average?
15. How many times did Mike lead the league in home runs?
16. How many Gold Gloves did he win in his career?
17. Off whom did Mike hit his 500th career home run?
18. Off what pitcher did Mike hit the division-clinching HR vs. Montreal in 1980?
19. In what inning did he hit that division-clinching HR vs. Montreal in 1980?
20. In Schmidt's four–home–run game vs. the Cubs, three of the homers were surrendered by a pair of brothers. Can you name this brother combination?

▶ EXTRA BASE HIT

Mike Schmidt was inducted into the Baseball Hall of Fame in 1995. Who was the only other player to join him in his Hall of Fame class?

ANSWERS

1. Roger Freed, who was a Phillies outfielder from 1971 to 1972. Freed batted .221 in 191 games.
2. In the second round. Schmidt was the 30th pick overall.
3. With their number–one pick that year, the sixth pick overall, the Phillies selected right–handed pitcher Roy Thomas. Thomas never played for the Phillies. He was involved in a trade with the White Sox for Jim Kaat, and eventually made it

to the majors with Houston in 1977. He spent eight seasons in the big leagues, winning 20 games and losing 11.

4. That was George Brett, who went to Kansas City as the 29th pick, one spot ahead of Schmidt.

5. His name was Tony Lucadello. Schmidt was not a hot prospect during his high school career. In his book *Clearing the Bases,* Schmidt writes that Lucadello was "the only major league scout that even knew I was alive." When the Phils drafted him out of college, Lucadello signed Schmidt for $32,500.

6. Schmidt attended Ohio University in Athens, Ohio. He was a walk-on who later blossomed into a two-time All-American.

7. Architecture was his major.

8. Technically, it was against the Reading Phillies. Shortly after he signed, Schmidt played shortstop for the big club in an exhibition at Reading. He hit a game-winner in the ninth. His first home run in a major league contest came against the Montreal Expos on September 16, 1972.

9. That first career homer came off Montreal lefty Balor Moore. It was a three-run shot to give the Phillies a 3-1 victory.

10. Jim Bunning at double-A Reading, where Schmidt spent a half-season in '71.

11. It was a bunt single on May 25, 1989 in the eighth inning of a game against the Dodgers in L.A.

12. He drew a walk against Terry Mulholland of the Giants.

13. In 132 games, Schmidt hit .193 in 1973, his first full season in the majors.

14. Mike had a lifetime batting average of .267

15. Mike led the National League a record eight times.

16. His 10 Gold Gloves are the most by a third baseman in NL history.

17. That would be the Pirates' Don Robinson on April 18, 1987 at Pittsburgh's Three Rivers Stadium.

18. It was the "Bahnsen Burner," Stan Bahnsen, who with the loss dropped to 7-6 on the year.

19. It was the top half of the 11th. One out, Pete Rose on first, in a 4-4 tie. Tug McGraw retired the Expos in order in the home half, and the Phillies were on their way to the playoffs.

20. They were Rick and Paul Reuschel. Rick was the starting pitcher that day. He gave up Schmidt's first two homers,

a two–run shot in the fifth inning, and a seventh–inning solo. His brother Paul came on in relief in the 10th, and gave up Schmidt's fourth home run of the day. It was a two–run bomb to put the Phillies ahead, 17-15. They eventually won, 18-16.

▶ EXTRA BASE HIT

Phillies legend Richie Ashburn, who was elected by the Veterans Committee. Schmidt was elected on the first ballot, the 26th player in history to be a first–ballot Hall of Famer. That weekend, Phillies fans painted Cooperstown red.

12

Who Am I?

This is much like the scoreboard puzzle game played between innings at the ballpark. Try to guess the identity of the Phillies players, past and present, based on the clues given below. There's a broadcaster you'll be asked to identify as well. How many clues will you need? In honor of Steve Carlton, there are 32 "Who Am I?" quizzes.

► 1

I attended Michigan State on a basketball scholarship.

I was the first Phillies pitcher to start an All-Star Game.

In my only World Series start, I gave up a 10th-inning HR to Joe DiMaggio.

I posted a streak of six consecutive 20-win seasons.

I once pitched 28 complete games in a row.

► 2

I originally signed as a catcher out of junior college.

I once played in a club-record 730 consecutive games.

I once fouled-off 14 pitches in a row in one at-bat.

I hit .300 in seven straight seasons, and got more hits than any player in the decade of the '50s.

I am the Phillies' only two-time batting champion.

▶ 3

I hit 20 or more HRs in each of my first six seasons with the
   Phillies.

I was the first Phillie to homer in five straight games.

I used a 40–ounce bat and once hit a ball an estimated 529 feet.

I had two tours of duty with the Phillies; in between I became
   MVP of the American League.

I am a native of Wampum, Pennsylvania.

▶ 4

I was born in Anchorage, Alaska.

Converted to a starting pitcher, I reached double-figure win
   totals five times in eight-plus seasons with the Phillies.

I am the only pitcher in team history to record 15 or more strikeouts in a game three times.

I am the last Phillie to lead the National League in strikeouts.

I became the fifth pitcher in major league history to strike out
   300 batters in consecutive seasons.

An ardent supporter of ALS research, I named my eldest son
   Gehrig.

▶ 5

I was originally drafted by the L.A. Dodgers, but did not sign.

My first major league hit was a grand slam.

I was the first Phillie since 1932 to notch 200 hits, 30 home runs,
   and 100 RBI in the same season.

I was the third player in team history to homer in five straight
   games.

I played for the U.S.A. in the inaugural World Baseball Classic.

I was the first Phillies second baseman with multiple 100 RBI
   seasons.

▶ 6

Born in Chicago, I was called up by the Phillies at age 19.

I was twice runner-up for National League MVP honors.

A four-time All-Star, I had three seasons of at least 30 HRs and
   100 RBI.

In '77, Mike Schmidt and I combined to hit 77 HRs.

These days you may catch me hanging around my barbeque pit at Citizens Bank Park.

▶ 7

I once had a streak of 26 consecutive stolen bases.

In 2007, I became the first Phillie in 25 years to have three consecutive multi-steal games.

I once had hits in seven consecutive at-bats.

As a Phillies AAA farmhand, I was once named the International League MVP.

My first career walk-off HR came on my own figurine day at Citizens Bank Park.

I am a native of Wailuku, Hawaii.

▶ 8

I am only the second Phillie in team history to have eight straight seasons of 20 or more home runs.

I am the last Phillie to lead the league in outfield assists.

I hold the Phillies' club record for most RBI in the month of April.

I once hit two homers in a playoff game.

I am a former winner of the Golden Spikes Award, given annually to the nation's top amateur player.

The Phillies selected me with the number–one overall pick in the 1998 draft.

▶ 9

In 13 full seasons, I hit over .300 11 times.

I was the second player in MLB history to hit four HRs in one game.

I have a .346 career batting average, the third highest in MLB history.

As a Phillie, I won one batting title and two HR titles.

I haven't played for the Phillies in over 100 years, and yet I still rank in the top 10 in most of the franchise's offensive categories.

► 10

I am one of only three Phillies pitchers to win a Gold Glove.

I am the only Phillie since 1917 to lead the league in ERA.

As a Phillie, I won 20 or more games five times.

I am the only Phillies pitcher to strike out 3,000 career batters.

My 329 victories are second among left–handers in MLB history.

I was the first pitcher in MLB history to win four Cy Young
    Awards, and the only Cy Young winner to pitch for a
    last–place team.

► 11

I hold the Phillies' club record for consecutive scoreless innings
    pitched by a reliever (33 innings).

My own throwing error led to the end of that scoreless innings
    streak.

I struck out two in the bottom of the 10th to earn the save in
    Game 5 of the '93 National League Championship Series.

I pitched for the Phillies in both the '83 and '93 World Series.

I've also served the Phillies as a minor league pitching coach,
    and most recently as a broadcaster.

► 12

I was one of the youngest players in team history when I made
    my debut at age 17.

Primarily an infielder, I also pitched in four games for the
    Phillies.

I never hit higher than .299 as a regular, but one season I
    clouted 21 homers and drove in 92 runs.

I am the only Phillie named as a starter in the All-Star Game at
    two different positions.

Jimmy Rollins is the only Phillies shortstop to hit more career
    homers than I did.

I was the captain of the 1950 "Whiz Kids."

▶ 13

I graduated with a degree in speech from the University of Iowa.

I was once the radio voice of the Class AAA Hawaii Islanders of the Pacific Coast League.

I have had the pleasure of broadcasting the first game in the history of three different ballparks.

I have called six no-hitters in my career.

I called every one of Mike Schmidt's 548 home runs. They were all "outta here!"

▶ 14

As a rookie, I was the club's lone representative on the NL All-Star team.

In my 4,000th career at-bat, I hit a home run.

I am only the second Phillie to become a member of baseball's 30/30 club.

I am fourth on the franchise's all-time steals list.

I was the first Phillies shortstop to score 100 runs in back-to-back seasons.

I was the first Phillies shortstop to win the Gold Glove Award in back-to-back seasons.

I was the first National Leaguer since Willie Mays to have 20 doubles, 20 triples, 20 homers, and 20 stolen bases in the same season.

▶ 15

I began and also finished my career in the American League, but along the way I spent 10 seasons with the Phillies.

A three-time All-Star, I was once runner-up in the voting for National League MVP.

I hit 23 or more HRs four times, knocked in 100 or more runs twice, and led the league in triples twice.

I played more games than any Phillies outfielder in the decade of the '60s.

I had two All-Star Game hits in my career, but one was a walk-off HR.

► 16

I was the first Phillie to have a multi-HR game in the World Series.

I twice led the NL in hits, and once set an MLB record for plate appearances.

I hit .300 three times; in one of those seasons I batted .400 into June.

I was the first Phillies outfielder to win a Silver Slugger Award.

I was named in the Mitchell Report on steroid use in baseball.

► 17

I hit .300 four times as a Phillie, and finished in the top 10 in batting twice.

In 10 years in the majors, I hit exactly 100 home runs, and had a career batting average of exactly .300.

I never got much credit for my glove, but I had a career fielding percentage of .994.

I batted .348 with an on-base percentage of .500 in the only World Series of my career.

I am a testicular cancer survivor, and was diagnosed after being struck in the groin by an errant throw from a teammate.

► 18

I was a two-time All-Star as a Phillie, and also won a Gold Glove and a Silver Slugger Award.

In eight-plus seasons with the Phils, I hit .300 six times including a career high of .335.

I was the third player in major league history to have seven straight seasons of 20 home runs and 20 stolen bases.

I was the fourth player in ML history to have seven straight seasons of 100 or more walks.

I was the first Phillies outfielder since Greg Luzinski to have consecutive seasons of 20 or more HRs.

I was the first Phillie to win the All-Star Game Home Run Derby.

▶ 19

I got the first hit by a Phillie at Citizens Bank Park.

I am one of two Phillies to hit 15 home runs in a single month.

I was the second player in ML history to have consecutive 40–home–run seasons in different leagues.

In my first season as a Phillie, I led the NL in home runs. My total that year was one HR shy of what was then the franchise record.

I enjoyed two outstanding seasons with the Phillies in which I blasted a total of 89 homers and drove in a total of 236 runs.

I hit my 400th career HR at Citizens Bank Park.

▶ 20

My first major league hit was a home run.

As a Phillie, I had double-figure HR totals in six straight seasons.

One year, I homered in every ballpark in the National League.

One of the most popular Phillies of my era, I was also a Phillies coach and minor league manager.

I was the starting catcher for the NL in the 1949 All-Star Game.

I was great at handling a pitching staff and was the backbone of the "Whiz Kids."

▶ 21

I led the NL in innings pitched six times; in wins, complete games, and strikeouts five times.

For 65 years, I was the only Phils pitcher who could say that I won a World Series game.

I was the fourth pitcher ever enshrined in the Hall of Fame, and my 373 wins are tied for third on the all-time list.

I won 30 or more games in three straight seasons, and hold the Phillies' team records for lowest ERA and most innings pitched in a season.

I still hold the ML record, and probably always will, with 16 shutouts in 1916.

▶ 22

I was the first Phillie to hit an extra-inning, inside-the-park home run.

Twice I knocked in seven runs in a game.

I hit 30 or more home runs twice, and drove in 100 or more runs six times.

Ashburn is the only outfielder to play in more games for the Phillies than I did.

During much of my career as a Phillie, I was the only native Philadelphian on the team.

I hit more home runs than any outfielder in Phillies history.

▶ 23

I played 15 seasons with the Phillies, and later became a Phillies coach.

I got my 1,000th career hit at Connie Mack Stadium and my 2,000th career hit at the Vet.

I was clutch in a pinch, stroking 17 pinch hits one season—the fourth most in club history.

I was the first player in team history to hit an "ultimate" grand slam. (That's a game-winning grand slam when trailing by three in the last inning.)

I am in the top 10 on the Phillies' all-time lists for games, at-bats, and singles.

I played more games at second base than anyone in Phillies history.

▶ 24

In six-plus seasons with the Phillies, I hit 150 home runs and had 880 hits. I also won three Gold Glove Awards.

I am the youngest player in team history to drive in 100 runs in a season.

I am only the second Phillie to ever notch 30 homers, 40 doubles, 100 RBI, and 100 runs in a season.

On September 17, 2001, the night baseball resumed following the terrorist attacks on the World Trade Center and the Pentagon, I hit two home runs off four-time Cy Young Award–winner Greg Maddux.

A native of Indiana, I received scholarship offers to play college basketball.

► **25**

I didn't make the majors until I was 25 years old, and didn't become a regular until I was 28.

I still rank in the top 10 in many of the Phillies' offensive categories.

A left-handed hitter, I was known as the "Babe Ruth of the NL," leading the league in homers four times.

Opponents employed one of the first defensive "shifts" against me with all three outfielders positioned between the right–field line and center field.

No Phillies center fielder ever had more home runs or RBI in a season than I did.

► **26**

I was once cut from my high school baseball team.

I stole 20 or more bases nine times as a Phillie, and 10 or more in each of my 12 seasons with the team.

My career high for HRs in a season is four. I hit two of them in the same game.

Best known for my defense, I led the NL in fielding percentage six times.

I set a record by starting seven double plays in a World Series. I also hit .375 in that Series.

A five-time All-Star as a player, I also served the Phillies as third–base coach, and later as the team's manager.

► **27**

I was the first pitcher since Cy Young to win 100 games in each league. I also pitched no-hitters in both leagues.

In a three-year period, I averaged over 300 innings pitched.

I won 19 games, three years in a row.

I lost a bid to become Governor of Kentucky, but was elected to seats in Congress and the U.S. Senate. As a father of seven, Father's Day has always been special. But in 1964, it was absolutely perfect!

▶ 28

A left–handed pitcher, I retired the first 19 left–handed hitters I faced in the majors.

I had 160 strikeouts in my first 25 big league starts, the most by any lefty since 1981.

In my first career complete game, I struck out a career-high 15 batters.

I became the first Phillies pitcher since 1999 to win 15 games in a season in less than 30 starts.

I was victorious in four straight starts in the 2008 postseason.

▶ 29

I once delivered a pinch-hit home run and an extra-inning HR in the same game.

I share the Phillies' team record for most HRs in the month of September.

I am the only Phillie in history to have three consecutive 40–homer seasons.

I hold the MLB record for most home runs in a season by a second–year player.

I reached 100 career HRs faster than any player in Major League Baseball history.

I won the National League MVP Award in my first full season in the majors.

▶ 30

In the first of my three seasons with the Phillies, I went 12-5, with 30 saves and a 2.34 ERA.

I once had 29 saves for a Phillies team that finished in last place.

My 102 saves are the most in team history by a left–handed relief pitcher.

My single-season high of 43 saves was once the team record.

My teammate John Kruk once traded me his uniform number for two cases of beer.

Unfortunately, my last pitch as a Phillie was hit for a walk-off home run.

▶ 31

I was once involved in a trade for Mitch Williams.

I am the oldest Phillie to ever get a hit in a game.

I am the oldest Phillie to ever earn a pitching victory.

In my MLB debut, I beat the Phillies and my boyhood idol, Steve Carlton.

When I was 45 years old, I won 16 games, tying the record for most wins by a pitcher 45 years of age or older.

I was the winning pitcher in both of the Phillies' division-clinching victories in 2007 and 2008.

I am a native of Souderton, Pennsylvania and attended Saint Joseph's University in Philadelphia.

▶ 32

My 463 games are the third most of all time among Phillies pitchers.

I am fourth on the team's saves list—second among lefties.

My combined total of 143 wins and saves ranks second among Phillies relievers, one shy of the club record.

My real name is Frank, but everyone calls me by my nickname.

I finished 313 games for the Phillies, the most in club history. But I am best remembered for the one I finished on October 21, 1980.

ANSWERS   1. Robin Roberts; 2. Richie Ashburn; 3. Dick Allen; 4. Curt Schilling; 5. Chase Utley; 6. Greg Luzinski; 7. Shane Victorino; 8. Pat Burrell; 9. Ed Delahanty; 10. Steve Carlton; 11. Larry Andersen; 12. Granny Hamner; 13. Harry Kalas; 14. Jimmy Rollins; 15. Johnny Callison; 16. Lenny Dykstra; 17. John Kruk; 18. Bobby Abreu; 19. Jim Thome; 20. Andy Seminick; 21. Grover Cleveland Alexander; 22. Del Ennis; 23. Tony Taylor; 24. Scott Rolen; 25. Cy Williams; 26. Larry Bowa; 27. Jim Bunning; 28. Cole Hamels; 29. Ryan Howard; 30. Mitch Williams; 31. Jamie Moyer; 32. Tug McGraw

13

Trades

Now we will delve into the wonderful world of Phillies trades. Some have been real stinkers, trades that changed the course of the franchise for the worse. One looks back in amazement and wonders what the front office was thinking. And others were simply exchanges of equally bad players. But there were also some very smart moves that turned out to be absolute steals.

Match the player on the left with the player on the right for whom he was traded.

Naturally, these are not all straight-up, one-for-one deals, but each player was involved in the trade. In honor of the 1980 World Champs, there are 80 pairs listed.

► 1

1. Del Unser	a. Joe Morgan
2. Gary Matthews	b. John Wockenfuss
3. Willie Hernandez	c. Garry Maddox
4. Willie Montanez	d. Tug McGraw
5. Mike Krukow	e. Bill Campbell

► 2

1. Scott Rolen	a. Kevin Millwood
2. Vicente Padilla	b. Eric Milton
3. Mickey Morandini	c. Placido Polanco
4. Johnny Estrada	d. Doug Glanville
5. Carlos Silva	e. A player to be named

▶ **3**

1. Tim McCarver	a. Tim McCarver
2. Cookie Rojas	b. Curt Flood
3. Larry Hisle	c. John Bateman
4. Dick Allen	d. Dave Cash
5. Ken Brett	e. Tommy Hutton

▶ **4**

1. Curt Schilling	a. Billy McMillon
2. Darren Daulton	b. Curt Schilling
3. Ryne Sandberg	c. Jeff Brantley
4. Jason Grimsley	d. Omar Daal
5. Ricky Bottalico	e. Ivan DeJesus

▶ **5**

1. Manny Trillo	a. Von Hayes
2. George Vukovich	b. Von Hayes
3. Jerry Williard	c. Kyle Abbott
4. Julio Franco	d. Von Hayes
5. Jay Baller	e. Von Hayes
6. Von Hayes	f. Von Hayes

▶ **6**

1. Jim Bunning	a. Oscar Gamble
2. Don Cardwell	b. Steve Carlton
3. Rick Wise	c. Don Money
4. Johnny Callison	d. Gary Matthews
5. Bob Walk	e. Tony Taylor

▶ **7**

1. Juan Samuel	a. John Kruk
2. Steve Bedrosian	b. Jeff Juden
3. Chris James	c. Desi Relaford
4. Mitch Williams	d. Len Dykstra
5. Terry Mulholland	e. Terry Mulholland

► 8

1. Ferguson Jenkins	a. Johnny Callison
2. Wally Post	b. Jim Bunning
3. Gene Freese	c. Bob Buhl
4. Don Demeter	d. Bill White
5. Art Mahaffey	e. Tony Gonzalez
6. Bucky Walters	f. Spud Davis

► 9

1. Marlon Byrd	a. Dan Plesac
2. Cliff Politte	b. Endy Chavez
3. John Mabry	c. Kent Bottenfield
4. Bruce Chen	d. Turk Wendell
5. Ron Gant	e. Jeremy Giambi

► 10

1. Jack Sanford	a. Alvin Dark
2. Richie Ashburn	b. Gene Conley
3. Andy Seminick	c. Chuck Klein
4. Stan Lopata	d. Ruben Gomez
5. Ethan Allen	e. Smoky Burgess

► 11

1. Kevin Stocker	a. Mark Whiten
2. Dave Hollins	b. Tommy Greene
3. Jeff Parrett	c. Heathcliff Slocumb
4. Glenn Wilson	d. Bobby Abreu
5. Ruben Amaro Jr.	e. Dale Murphy
6. Jim Vatcher	f. Phil Bradley

► 12

1. Jason Michaels	a. Tadahito Iguchi
2. Michael Bourn	b. Billy Wagner
3. Brandon Duckworth	c. Eric Bruntlett
4. Geoff Geary	d. Brad Lidge
5. Michael Dubee	e. Arthur Rhodes

► 13

1. Larry Bowa
2. Dick Ruthven
3. Don Money
4. Bake McBride
5. Jay Johnstone

a. Jim Kaat
b. Jim Lonborg
c. Sid Monge
d. Rawley Eastwick
e. Ivan DeJesus

► 14

1. Adam Eaton
2. Placido Polanco
3. Bobby Abreu
4. Gavin Floyd
5. Jim Thome

a. Matt Smith
b. Aaron Rowand
c. Andy Ashby
d. Ugueth Urbina
e. Freddy Garcia

► 15

1. Al Holland
2. Keith Moreland
3. Ron Reed
4. Ted Sizemore
5. Ozzie Virgil
6. Lonnie Smith

a. Milt Thompson
b. Bo Diaz
c. Manny Trillo
d. Kent Tekulve
e. Jerry Koosman
f. Mike Krukow

ANSWERS **1.** 1d, 2e, 3b, 4c, 5a; **2.** 1c, 2e, 3d, 4a, 5b;
3. 1c, 2a, 3e, 4b, 5d; **4.** 1d, 2a, 3e, 4b, 5c;
5. 1a, 2b, 3d, 4e, 5f, 6c; **6.** 1c, 2e, 3b, 4a, 5d;
7. 1d, 2e, 3a, 4b, 5c; **8.** 1c, 2e, 3a, 4b, 5d, 6f;
9. 1b, 2a, 3e, 4d, 5c; **10.** 1d, 2a, 3e, 4b, 5c;
11. 1d, 2a, 3e. 4f, 5c, 6b; **12.** 1e, 2d, 3b, 4c, 5a; **13.** 1e, 2a, 3b,
4c, 5d; **14.** 1c, 2d, 3a, 4e, 5b; **15.** 1d, 2f, 3e, 4c, 5a, 6b

14

Who Said It?

The Phillies have had more than their share of colorful characters over the years. Some of those characters have had a talent for delivering colorful quotes. Others have shown a talent for inserting their feet in their mouths. And then there are the players who can't help themselves, and love stirring the pot by delivering the controversial.

Below are some of the more memorable quotes ever uttered by a Phillie into a reporter's microphone or recorded on a notepad. In this quiz, try to match the line with the person by whom it was spoken.

1. "Philadelphia is the only place where you can experience the thrill of victory and the agony of reading about it in the paper."
   a. Scott Rolen
   b. Mike Schmidt
   c. Curt Schilling
   d. Mitch Williams

2. "Nobody's going to make a scrapgoat out of me."
   a. Paul Owens
   b. Danny Ozark
   c. Frank Lucchesi
   d. Jim Fregosi

3. "Trying to sneak a fastball past Aaron is like trying to sneak the sun past a rooster."
   a. Steve Carlton
   b. Curt Simmons
   c. Robin Roberts
   d. Gene Mauch

4. "I ain't no athlete lady, I'm a baseball player."
   a. John Kruk
   b. Len Dykstra
   c. Tug McGraw
   d. Jeff Stone

5. When asked which is better, grass or Astro-Turf, this player replied, "I don't know, I've never smoked Astro-Turf."
   a. Darren Daulton
   b. Lonnie Smith
   c. Jay Johnstone
   d. Tug McGraw

6. Commenting on the team's ace pitcher, he said, "Every fifth day he's a horse, the rest of the time he's a horse's ass."
   a. Mitch Williams
   b. Ed Wade
   c. Dallas Green
   d. Larry Bowa

7. Commenting on a player who enjoyed alcoholic beverages, this manager said, "His problem isn't with high fastballs, it's with fast highballs."
   a. Gene Mauch
   b. Dallas Green
   c. Lee Elia
   d. Mayo Smith

8. In sizing up the NL East race before the season, he said, "I think we're the team to beat."
   a. Brett Myers
   b. Larry Bowa
   c. Jimmy Rollins
   d. Jim Thome

9. "There's only 18 inches between a pat on the back and a kick in the butt."
   a. Paul Owens
   b. Danny Ozark
   c. Frank Lucchesi
   d. Jim Fregosi

10. On the subject of his weight, this Phillie once quipped, "I need two hands to haul ass."
    a. Jon Lieber
    b. John Kruk
    c. Ryan Howard
    d. Ryan Madson

11. In stating the reason for his sudden retirement, this manager said, "I'm 49 and I want to live to be 50."
    a. Ben Chapman
    b. Kaiser Wilhelm
    c. Nick Leyva
    d. Eddie Sawyer

12. "Even Napoleon had his Watergate."
    a. Paul Owens
    b. Danny Ozark
    c. Frank Lucchesi
    d. Jim Fregosi

13. "Every time I'm at the plate, I'm trying to hit a home run. I swing as hard as I can. I'm not a guy who's going to single and steal second."
    a. Greg Luzinski
    b. Ryan Howard
    c. Matt Stairs
    d. Joe Blanton

14. To a reporter who questioned whether he got mad enough at his players, this manager said, "Why don't you come into my office later; I'll show you just how mad I can get."
    a. Jim Fregosi
    b. Terry Francona

c. Dallas Green

d. Charlie Manuel

15. "Yes we can" (which became the team's rallying cry).
   a. Dave Cash
   b. Jimmy Rollins
   c. Tug McGraw
   d. Larry Bowa

16. On the pitch that clinched the '80 World Series: "It was the slowest fastball in history. It took 97 years to get there."
   a. Pete Rose
   b. Larry Bowa
   c. Tug McGraw
   d. Dallas Green

17. "Philly fans, and I might get flack for this, are front-runners. They're on your side when you're doing good, but when you're doing bad, they're against you."
   a. Jimmy Rollins
   b. Billy Wagner
   c. Larry Bowa
   d. Kenny Lofton

18. "I don't care if you throw at me. Just throw at my ribs, not at my head. That's all I ask."
   a. Aaron Rowand
   b. Shane Victorino
   c. Pete Rose
   d. Chase Utley

19. On the reasons he crashed into the wall to make a game-saving catch, breaking his nose and cheekbone in the process, this Phillie said, "For who? My teammates. For what? To win the game."
   a. Lenny Dykstra
   b. Hack Wilson
   c. Glenn Wilson
   d. Aaron Rowand

20. "World Champions. World F@#%in' Champions!!"
    a. Brett Myers
    b. Pat Burrell
    c. Charlie Manuel
    d. Chase Utley

ANSWERS   **1**.b, **2**.c, **3**.b, **4**.a, **5**.d, **6**.b, **7**.a, **8**.c, **9**.c, **10**.b, **11**.d, **12**.b, **13**.c, **14**.d, **15**.a, **16**.c, **17**.a, **18**.b, **19**.d, **20**.d

15

Owners and Team Presidents

We will now turn our attention to the guys at the top, the people who have owned and operated the club. When it comes to team owners, there's always a trickle–down effect. Winning and losing start at the top. If there isn't strong leadership there, the effects are felt on the field. Conversely, if the right decisions are made, the results are usually seen in the win column. That has certainly been true of the Phillies. The men who've run the franchise over its long history have been an eclectic mix. One was the first professional ballplayer. Another was once a stadium ticket-taker. One, a former New York police commissioner. A couple have been Ivy League grads. Yet another, a promotional wiz who grew up in the game. They have all run the franchise with differing results.

1. Which team president was captain of the baseball team at Yale?
2. Which team president, while vice president of operations, oversaw the creation of the Phillie Phanatic?
3. Who was the very first owner of the Phillies?
4. Which Phillies owner was banned from baseball for betting on the Phillies?
5. What Phillies owner was the first professional player?

6. Which team president was the youngest in major league history?
7. Name the Phillies owner who sold his cigar company for three billion dollars.
8. Which team president's father was GM of the Cincinnati Reds, and later president of the National League?
9. Name the Phillies owner who was a former New York City police commissioner.
10. Which owner assumed control of the Phillies when his wife inherited shares of the franchise?
11. Which man had the longest tenure running the Phillies?
12. How much did the group headed by Bill Giles pay for the Phillies?
13. Which team president graduated with an MBA from Penn?
14. Can you name the current Phillies owners?
15. Who owned the Phillies when they won the World Series in 1980?

▶ EXTRA BASE HIT

Who was the team president who rose from ballpark ticket-taker?

1. That would be Ruly Carpenter, who also played football at Yale. He later served as an assistant baseball coach at the University of Delaware.
2. It was under promotional genius Bill Giles' watch that the Phanatic was born.
3. His name was Alfred J. Reach, and he owned the club from 1883 to 1902. Reach, a former player, made a fortune in the sporting goods business, manufacturing baseball equipment. Until Ruly Carpenter came along, no team president had a better winning percentage than Reach.
4. William D. Cox, who owned the Phillies in 1943. Cox was a meddlesome owner who was constantly at odds with his manager, Bucky Harris. Eventually he fired Harris. So Bucky took his revenge by leaking to the media that Cox bet on the Phillies. Commissioner Kenesaw Mountain Landis promptly banned Cox for life.

5. In 1865, Al Reach signed a contract to play for a team called the Philadelphia Athletics. Until then baseball was an amateur game. Reach became the first to sign a contract and earn a salary. He was paid $1,000.

6. Bob Carpenter Jr. was 28 years old when his father bought the club and named him president. Carpenter took over the reins of a floundering franchise and gave it stability. Nowadays we'd call it "changing the culture." Although the team didn't win much under his direction, Carpenter's shining moment came with the pennant-winning team of 1950. Between himself and his son, Ruly, the Phillies were under the Carpenters' stewardship for four decades.

7. John S. Middleton, one of the members of the current ownership group.

8. Bill Giles' father, Warren Giles, was general manager of the Reds from 1937 to 1951, before spending 18 years as National League president.

9. William F. Baker, of Baker Bowl fame. He continued to live in New York City even after he was running the club, commuting back and forth to Philadelphia. Baker owned the team from 1913 until his death in 1930.

10. His name was Gerald Nugent. Nugent was working for the club as William Baker's assistant when he married Baker's secretary, Mae Mallon. When Baker died, he left shares in the team to Mae Nugent. When Baker's wife died, she left her shares to Mrs. Nugent and the Nugents' son. Those shares, coupled with some that Nugent had purchased on his own, gave him 51 percent of the team.

11. Bob Carpenter Jr., who ran the Phillies for 29 years.

12. The Giles group paid 30 million dollars to the Carpenter family, which had paid $400,000 in 1943.

13. David Montgomery earned an MBA from the University of Pennsylvania's Wharton School of Business. He then joined the Phillies sales office, selling group and season tickets.

14. They are Montgomery, Giles, Claire S. Betz, Alexander K. Buck, J. Mahlon Buck Jr., William C. Buck, and John S. Middleton.

15. The Carpenter family, under the direction of Ruly Carpenter. Ruly presided over the golden era of Phillies baseball as he guided the franchise from '72 to '81. The mid to late 1970s was the franchise's most successful, culminating with the

World Series title in 1980. Carpenter abruptly sold the team
the following year after becoming disillusioned with
escalating player salaries.

▶ EXTRA BASE HIT

You have to go back to the turn of the last century to find a story
like Billy Shettsline's. Shettsline worked his way up from ticket-
taker to the front office. He also spent five years in the dugout as
the team's manager before becoming team president from 1905 to
1908.

16

The Managers

When it comes to the subject of Phillies managers, Phillies fans have strong opinions, and usually they're in agreement that almost all of them have sucked. To be fair, most have gone to battle with inferior ammunition. The talent hand they were dealt was often not up to par. Many who've skippered the club have done so with disastrous results, and were every bit as bad as the fans' venom would suggest. Still, there have been some outstanding baseball men who've graced the Phillies dugout. They even won some games.

This section spotlights the men who've called the shots on the field.

1. Can you name the oldest manager in Phillies history?
2. Which Phillies manager, as a player, had the National League's highest single-season batting average?
3. On two occasions, GM Paul Owens took over as manager during a season. Who were the managers he succeeded?
4. Who is the only Phillies manager to win Manager of the Year honors?
5. Which Phillies manager was the son of a former Phillie?
6. Who is the last Philadelphia native to manage the Phillies?
7. Who was the Phillies' very first manager?
8. What was Eddie Sawyer's former profession?
9. Who is the winningest manager in Phillies history?

10. Which Phillies manager won the most games in a season?
11. Which Philles manager set a Japanese League record for HRs by an American?
12. Of Jim Fregosi's six seasons as Phils skipper, how many were winning seasons?
13. Name the only two managers to manage over 1,000 games with the Phillies.
14. Which Phillies manager was a Vaudeville performer?
15. Which ex-Phillies manager won the 1919 World Series with the Cincinnati Reds?
16. Which Phillies manager was a practicing dentist?
17. Can you name the Phillies manager who was born on Christmas Day?
18. Who is the only Phillies manager to have an unbeaten record?
19. Which Phillies manager was fired after the fewest games in a season?
20. Name the four former Phillies skippers who, after leaving the Phillies, won the World Series with other teams. (I've already spotted you the hardest one.)
21. What ex-Phillies manager went on to become the first manager of the expansion Montreal Expos?
22. What former Phillies manager, as skipper of the Brooklyn Dodgers, lost the pennant to the Phillies?
23. Which Phillies manager had a son who became an NFL head coach?
24. Which Phillies manager was an all-conference basketball player at the University of Delaware?
25. During his playing days, which Phillies manager was once traded for Hall of Fame pitcher Nolan Ryan?

► EXTRA BASE HIT

Name the six men who guided the Phillies to National League pennants.

ANSWERS

1. Charlie Manuel, who was born on January 4, 1944, is the oldest man to skipper the Phillies. He and Steve O'Neill, who

managed the team from 1952 to 1954, were both 60 years old when they were first named as Phillies Manager. Manuel, however, turned 61 before he managed his first game. Paul Owens was 60 in his final season in the dugout.

2. That's Hall of Famer Hugh Duffy. Duffy hit .440 in 1894 for Boston. He was one of the great players of the pre-1900 era. In his 17 years, the outfielder had a career average of .324 and 2,284 hits. He wasn't so great as a manager. Duffy led the Phillies from 1904 to 1906. His first Phillies team lost 100 games. In three seasons as Phils manager, the team finished eighth, fourth, and fourth. In eight seasons as a big league manager, Duffy had only two teams with winning records.

3. "The Pope" fired Frank Lucchesi in '72, and assumed the reins in the dugout. Newly appointed as general manager, Owens wanted to find out first–hand just what kind of players he had. In '83, with the team in first place but just a game over .500, Owens fired Pat Corrales, and again inserted himself in the managerial role. Under Owens, the Phils went on to win the NL pennant. The following season he gave up his GM duties to stay on as manager, but the team finished fourth and Owens went back to the front office as an assistant to team president Bill Giles.

4. Would you believe Larry Bowa? The former All-Star shortstop was voted 2001 National League Manager of the Year by the Baseball Writers Association of America. The 2001 season was Bowa's first as Phillies manager, and he guided the team to an 86-76 record and a second–place finish.

5. The man that Bowa succeeded, Terry Francona. Terry's father, Tito, who had a 15-year big league career, played for the Phillies in 1967. A first baseman/outfielder, he batted .205 in 27 games. Terry managed the team from 1997 to 2000. His squads never had much talent and never finished higher than third, twice finishing last.

6. That would be Lee Elia. Once a three-sport star at Olney High School, Elia replaced John Felske midway through the 1987 season. Late in '88, with the club at 60-92, Elia was fired.

7. His name was Bob Ferguson, and he didn't last very long. A player/manager, he was also the team's second baseman. After the Phillies lost 13 of their first 17 games, Ferguson was relieved of his managerial duties. He remained the second

baseman, hitting .258 while leading the league with 88 errors. Ferguson had one of the more interesting nicknames in franchise history. He was known as "Death to Flying Things."

8. Eddie Sawyer wasn't called "The Professor" for nothing. At one time he was indeed a college professor. The scholarly Sawyer graduated with honors from Ithaca College, and also earned a master's degree from Cornell. After a brief retirement from his minor league playing career, Sawyer took a teaching post at Ithaca. He returned to the game as a player/manager and, for a while, continued to teach in the off-season.

9. That's "The Little General," Gene Mauch. He had 645 victories, the most of any Phillies manager. But no pennants. Even so, some consider him the finest manager the Phillies ever had.

10. Danny Ozark, who twice won 101. Ozark skippered the Phils from 1973 to 1979. In both '76 and '77, he guided the Phils to records of 101-61 and two division crowns. The 101 victories are the Phillies' single-season record.

11. In 1980, Charlie Manuel hit 48 home runs for the Kintetsu Buffaloes of the Japanese Pacific League. At the time, it was an American record for Japanese baseball. The year before, he became the first American to win the league's MVP award.

12. There was just one. That was in 1993, when the Phillies went 97-65. Fregosi skippered the Phillies from 1991 to 1996. His overall record was 431-463.

13. They are Gene Mauch and Danny Ozark. Mauch managed 1,331; Ozark, 1,105.

14. Charlie "Red" Dooin performed with an Irish comedy act called "His Last Night Out." Dooin was Phils manager from 1910 to 1914.

15. That was Pat Moran, who took the 1915 Phils to the franchise's first World Series. Four years later, he was back in the Fall Classic with the Reds. This time he won it all when the "Black Sox" threw the series.

16. James "Doc" Prothro, who managed the Phillies from 1939 to 1941. Prothro graduated from the University of Tennessee Dental School and started practicing dentistry in 1917. As a major league player in the 1920s, and later as a minor league manager, he continued his practice in the off-season. Getting

his Phillies teams to play was like pulling teeth. Prothro lost 320 games in three seasons while managing three of the worst teams in Phillies history. He has the worst winning percentage of anyone who managed the team for more than one season.

17. Ben Chapman was on born December 25, 1908. Chapman served as Phillies manager from 1945 to 1948. He may have been born on Christmas Day, but he hardly showed goodwill toward man when that man was Jackie Robinson. Chapman's racial taunting of Major League Baseball's first African-American player was so bad that the Phillies skipper was reprimanded by NL president Ford Frick.

18. It's true, there is a guy with a spotless record. His name was Andy Cohen. Of course, he only managed one game. It was the second game of the 1960 season. After Eddie Sawyer abruptly quit following the season opener, the Phillies hired Gene Mauch to replace him. But before Mauch could get to Philadelphia, the Phillies had another game to play. Cohen, then a Phils coach, had to manage game number two. Under his direction, the Phillies beat the Cincinnati Reds. It was Cohen's one and only game as manager. His 1-0 record makes him the only unbeaten manager in Phillies history!

19. That was Nick Leyva, who was fired after 13 games in 1991. The Phillies lost nine of those first 13.

20. I gave you one in question 15—Pat Moran. The other three were Bucky Harris, Mayo Smith, and Terry Francona. Moran, of course, lost the 1915 Series with the Phils, but won in 1919, the series made famous by the "Black Sox" scandal. Harris managed the Phillies in 1943 but didn't make it past July before being fired. In '47, he won it all with the Yankees. Smith was the Phils skipper from 1955 to 1958, his first big league managerial job. In 1968, he led the Tigers to the title. Francona managed some lousy Phillies teams from 1997 to 2000. But in 2004, he took over the Red Sox and guided them to that franchise's first World Series championship in 86 years. Francona and the Red Sox won it again in 2007. He is the only manager in history to win his first eight World Series games.

21. That's Gene Mauch. The Phils fired him during the 1968 season. The following year he was hired to lead the Expos. Mauch managed in Montreal for the next seven years.

22. This answer was revealed in the section on the 1950 team. It's Burt Shotton, who managed the Phillies from 1928 to 1933 and had a winning percentage of .403.
23. That was the dentist, "Doc" Prothro. Football fans from the 1970s will remember his son, Tommy, who coached the L.A. Rams and the San Diego Chargers. Tommy Prothro was a big-time college coach as well, winning the Rose Bowl with UCLA in 1966.
24. The player was Dallas Green. The six–foot–five Green made All-Middle Atlantic Conference in basketball for the Delaware Blue Hens.
25. It was Jim Fregosi. Following the 1971 season, Fregosi, then an 11-year veteran and six-time All-Star, was traded by the Angels to the New York Mets for four players. Included in the deal was a young pitcher who had yet to live up to his potential named Nolan Ryan. But that's when Ryan's career took off. In his first season with the Angels, he won 19 games and was on his way to becoming one of the game's greats.

▶ EXTRA BASE HIT

In order they are: Pat Moran, 1915; Eddie Sawyer, 1950; Dallas Green, 1980; Paul Owens, 1983; Jim Fregosi, 1993; and, last but not least, Charlie Manuel in 2008. As you know, Manuel and Green are the only ones to win the World Series.

17

All-Stars

It's a midseason tradition in baseball that began in 1933. The All-Star Game is one of the highlights of the season, looked forward to by baseball fans everywhere. Over the years, the Phillies have been well represented, as dozens of members of the hometown nine have been named to the National League squad.

The most players to represent the Phillies at a single mid-summer classic is five, and that's been done on four occasions.

They've had starting pitchers, winning pitchers, managers, rookie selections, and at least one All-Star Game hero. Below is a star-studded lineup of trivia pertaining to Phillies in the All-Star Game.

1. Who was the last Phillie to be the winning pitcher in an All-Star Game?
2. Who was the first Phillie to be the winning pitcher in an All-Star Game? (This is a toughie.)
3. Who was the last Phillies pitcher to start an All-Star game?
4. Which Phillies pitcher made the most career All-Star Game starts?
5. When was the last time the All-Star Game was played in Philadelphia?
6. Who was the first Phillies manager to win an All-Star Game?
7. Who was the last?
8. There are two Phillies who share the honor of being the first Phillies to start in an All-Star Game. Can you name them?

9. Which Phillies have won the All-Star Home Run Derby? (It doesn't get easier than that!)
10. How many home runs did Mike Schmidt hit in All-Star Game competition?
11. How many Phillies have hit All-Star Game home runs?
12. Who is the only Phillie to be named MVP of the All-Star Game?
13. Who was the last Phillie to start at first base?
14. Who was the last Phillies rookie to make an All-Star team? (Hint: He's a position player.)
15. Who was the last rookie pitcher from the Phillies to make an All-Star team?

▶ EXTRA BASE HIT

How many times was Mike Schmidt selected to the All-Star team?

▶ WALK-OFF SINGLE

Who is the last Phillie to be the losing pitcher in an All-Star Game?

ANSWERS

1. Heathcliff Slocumb was the last Phillies pitcher to earn an All-Star Game victory. Slocumb was the winning pitcher in 1995 in Arlington, Texas, as the NL beat the AL, 3-2. Slocumb got the final two outs of the seventh inning. Then, after Jeff Conine hit a go-ahead home run to make it 3-2 NL, Slocumb started the eighth and retired one batter before being removed after surrendering a base hit. It was enough to earn the win.

2. I wouldn't expect many fans to know this one. His name was Ken Raffensberger, and he won the 1944 game at Forbes Field in Pittsburgh. He wasn't the first pitcher to represent the Phils in the game. That was Bucky Walters in 1937. But Raffensberger was the first to be winning pitcher. The NL won 7-1, with Raffensberger pitching two shutout innings. The southpaw pitched for the Phillies from 1943 to 1947, and had an overall record of 119-154, with a 3.60 ERA. In '44, despite his selection as an All-Star, Raffensberger finished 13-20 and led the league in losses.

3. Curt Schilling was last. Schill was on the hill to start the 1999 All-Star Game at Fenway Park in Boston, the last Phillie to be the starting pitcher in the midsummer classic. Schilling was 13-4 at the All-Star Break to earn the nod. He wound up as the losing pitcher after giving up two runs in two innings of work.

4. Robin Roberts made five All-Star Game starts in his career. Roberts was selected to the NL squad seven times, and he is tied with Steve Carlton for most career selections among Phillies pitchers.

5. On July 9, 1996, at Veterans Stadium. It was the second time the Vet had played host; the other was in the Bicentennial year of 1976. It was also the fourth time the game was played in Philadelphia. Shibe Park was the game's site in 1943 and 1952. The NL shut out the AL, 6-0, in '96. Norristown, Pennsylvania native Mike Piazza of the Dodgers hit a home run and was named the MVP. Pitcher Ricky Bottalico was the lone Phillies All-Star that year. Incidentally, the last game in Philly was also the last game the National League won.

6. The man who guided the "Whiz Kids" to the '50 pennant, Eddie Sawyer. One of the perks of managing a pennant-winner is that the following season you get to manage the All-Star team. Sawyer led the '51 NL stars to an 8-3 win at Briggs Stadium in Detroit, becoming the first Phils manager to notch an All-Star win.

7. Jim Fregosi, who skippered the '94 NL stars to an 8-7 win at Three Rivers Stadium in Pittsburgh. In fact, every Phillies manager who has led the NL squad has won the game. Gene Mauch in '65 and Dallas Green in '81 are the others.

8. Outfielder Chuck Klein and shortstop Dick Bartell were the first Phillies to start in an All-Star Game, earning starting spots in the inaugural game in 1933 at Chicago's Comiskey Park. Klein started in right field and batted third. He was the first Phillie to bat in an All-Star Game and the first to get a hit. Bartell was seventh in the NL batting order. He went 0–for–2 with a strikeout.

9. They are Bobby Abreu and Ryan Howard. Abreu won it in 2005, Howard in 2006.

10. In all of his All-Star Games, Schmidt went deep only once. He hit a home run off Rollie Fingers in 1981 at Municipal Stadium in Cleveland.

11. Well, we've already established that Schmidty is one. He happens to be the last Phillie to homer in an All-Star Game. In reverse chronological order, the others are: Greg Luzinski, 1977, at Yankee Stadium; Richie Allen, 1967, in Anaheim; and Johnny Callison, 1964, at Shea Stadium.

12. It was Johnny Callison in 1964. That Callison home run happened to be a dramatic, game-winning, three-run shot in the bottom of the ninth to give the NL a 7-4 victory at Shea. It was served up by Boston's Dick Radatz. The walk-off earned Callison MVP honors.

13. That would be John Kruk in 1993, at Camden Yards in Baltimore. Kruk had a rough time facing the American League's Randy Johnson, whiffing in the third inning. On the night, Kruk was 0-for-3 with two strikeouts.

14. It was Jimmy Rollins in 2001, at Seattle. He was also the Phils' lone representative. Cole Hamels made it in 2007, his first full season in the majors, but he did not qualify as a rookie. In that 2001 game, Rollins walked in his only at-bat, and then stole second. He's the answer to another bit of Phillies All-Star Game trivia. Rollins is the last Phillie to steal a base in the All-Star Game.

15. That was Tyler Green in 1995. He pitched a scoreless inning in the National League's win at Arlington, Texas, even striking out Twins star Kirby Puckett. It was the same game in which Heathcliff Slocumb emerged as the winning pitcher. Green was one of five Phillies on the NL team that year. It was the highlight of his career. A former first-round pick, he was done by '97 after going 18-25 with a 5.16 ERA in 70 games.

▶ EXTRA BASE HIT

Mike Schmidt was a 12-time All-Star in his illustrious career. No other Phillie comes close. Nine times, Schmidt was voted a starter, including 1989, when he was elected to start but did not play because he had retired in May of that season.

▶ WALK-OFF SINGLE

It was Brad Lidge, who got the loss in the 2008 game at Yankee Stadium. Lidge gave up a sacrifice fly in the bottom of the 15th inning to give the American League a 4-3 win.

18

The Postseason

Up until October 2008, the Phillies postseasons were marked mostly by heartbreak. Not anymore. Phillies fans can now say they are the two-time World Series champs, and doesn't that sound so much better? Happiness to go along with that heartbreak. But there has been heartbreak, especially in the postseason. As you bask in the afterglow of the 2008 title, meander down memory lane through the highs, and the lows, of the Phillies' history in October.

Key: NLDS=National League Division Series; NLCS=National League Championship Series; WS=World Series

► 1

Who came on in relief to give up a series-turning grand slam in the second game of the 2007 NLDS?

  a. Kyle Lohse
  b. Chad Durbin
  c. J.C. Romero
  d. Brett Myers

► 2

Who was the Phillies' starting pitcher in Game 1 of the 1980
World Series?

  a. Steve Carlton
  b. Dick Ruthven
  c. Bob Walk
  d. Marty Bystrom

► 3

Who was the Phillies' starting pitcher in Game 1 of the 1950
World Series?

  a. Jim Konstanty
  b. Bubba Church
  c. Russ Meyer
  d. Robin Roberts

► 4

Which Phillie hit .429 in the 1983 NLCS?

  a. Mike Schmidt
  b. Gary Matthews
  c. Gary Maddox
  d. Joe Morgan

► 5

Who was the first Phillies pitcher to earn a WS victory?

  a. Grover C. Alexander
  b. Erskine Mayer
  c. Eppa Rixey
  d. Robin Roberts

► 6

Who hit the game-winning home run in Game 1 of the 1983
World Series?

  a. Sixto Lezcano
  b. Garry Maddox
  c. Mike Schmidt
  d. Gary Matthews

► **7**

Which Phillie batted .400 in the 1980 NLCS?

a. Manny Trillo
b. Bake McBride
c. Bob Boone
d. Pete Rose

► **8**

Which sure-handed fielder dropped a fly ball that set up the series-winning run in the 1978 NLCS?

a. Larry Bowa
b. Mike Schmidt
c. Jerry Martin
d. Garry Maddox

► **9**

The Phillies beat Houston in five games to win the 1980 NLCS. How many of the games went extra innings?

a. One
b. Two
c. Four
d. All five

► **10**

Whose two-run HR provided the winning margin in the first game of the '80 NLCS?

a. Greg Luzinski
b. Mike Schmidt
c. Greg Gross
d. Pete Rose

► **11**

Match the player on the left with his place in Phillies postseason history.

1. Milt Thompson   a. Hit series-clinching double in NLCS
2. Mariano Duncan   b. Holds team record for most HRs in a
3. Lenny Dykstra   World Series

4. Garry Maddox   c. Had five RBI in a World Series game
5. Del Unser   d. Had two HRs and five RBI in a WS game
6. Ryan Howard   e. Scored series-winning run in NLCS
7. Shane Victorino   f. Holds team record for most hits in a WS
                     g. Hit the Phillies' only postseason grand slam

▶ 12

Other than Joe Carter's series-winning home run, what do you remember about the '93 World Series?

Match the game on the left with the event in which it occurred.

1. Game 1   a. Fregosi uses Ricky Jordan as designated hitter
2. Game 4   b. Schilling pitches first World Series shutout in Phils history
3. Game 6
4. Game 2   c. Eisenreich hits clutch three-run HR
5. Game 5   d. Game delayed 72 minutes due to rain.
6. Game 3   e. Dykstra hits two homers
                f. Mulholland gives up three-run first inning

▶ 13

You'd probably rather relive 1980. Match the game from the '80 World Series with the corresponding event.

1. Game 1   a. Four-run eighth propels Phillies to victory
2. Game 2   b. McGraw strikes out Wilson to end game
3. Game 3   c. Noles brushes back Brett
4. Game 4   d. Trillo has the game-winning hit
5. Game 5   e. Rose backs up Boone for second out in ninth
6. Game 6   f. McGraw is the loser in 10

▶ 14

What was the count on Willie Wilson when McGraw struck him right on out of there to end the '80 WS?

a. 0 and 2
b. 1 and 2
c. 2 and 2
d. 3 and 2

► **15**

What happened when in the 2007 NLDS?

1. Game 1
2. Game 2
3. Game 2

a. Rollins hits first lead-off HR in Phillies playoff history

b. Moyer starts, goes six strong innings, and gets no decision

c. Rowand and Burrell hit the first back-to-back HRs in Phillies playoff history

► **16**

Here's some trivia from October 7, 1977, better known as "Black Friday" (third game, 1977 NLCS vs. the Dodgers).

1. Bruce Froemming
2. Davey Lopes
3. Burt Hooton
4. Greg Luzinski
5. Jerry Martin
6. Bob Boone

a. Only Phillie with multiple hits

b. Couldn't come up with fly ball in ninth inning

c. Defensive replacement Ozark failed to use

d. Blew call at first base in ninth inning

e. Pitcher who became unnerved by fans.

f. Scored game-winning run

► **17**

Postseason pitching feats—see if you can hit them out of the park.

1. Dick Ruthven
2. John Denny
3. Steve Carlton
4. Curt Schilling
5. Tommy Greene

a. Won series-clincher in '93 NLCS

b. Only Phillie to strike out 10 in a WS game

c. Only Phillie to strike out 10 in an LCS game

d. Won series-clincher in '80 NLCS

e. Earned Phillies' only win of '83 WS

► **18**

Postseason award-winners:

1. Manny Trillo
2. Gary Matthews
3. Mike Schmidt
4. Curt Schilling

a. 1980 World Series MVP

b. 1993 NLCS MVP

c. 1983 NLCS MVP

d. 1980 NLCS MVP

▶ 19

Who is the only Phillie to be NLCS MVP and WS MVP in the same postseason?

▶ 20

Who is the only Phillie to hit a walk-off HR in a postseason game? (It was a pinch-hit, solo shot in the bottom of the 10th in the fourth game of the 1981 NLDS vs. Montreal.)

▶ 21

Whose home run in the top of the 10th inning won the fifth game of the '93 NLCS, giving the Phillies a 3-2 series lead over the Braves?

   a. Darren Daulton
   b. Lenny Dykstra
   c. Pete Incaviglia
   d. Dave Hollins

ANSWERS   **1**.a, **2**.c, **3**.a, **4**.b, **5**.a, **6**.b, **7**.d, **8**.d, **9**.c, **10**.a, **11**. 1c, 2f, 3b, 4a, 5e, 6d, 7g; **12**. 1a, 2e, 3f, 4c, 5b, 6d; **13**. 1b, 2a, 3f, 4c, 5d, 6e; **14**. b, **15**. 1c, 2a, 3b; **16**. 1d, 2f, 3e, 4b, 5c, 6a; **17**. 1d, 2e, 3b, 4c, 5a; **18**. 1d, 2c, 3a, 4b; **19**. Cole Hamels, 2008; **20**. George Vukovich, **21**. b

▶ 22

More Phillies postseason records:
   1. Who holds the Phillies record for most RBI in a postseason?
   2. Who holds the Phillies record for most pitching victories in a single postseason?
   3. Who holds the Phillies record for most hits by a pitcher in a postseason game?
   4. Which Phillie was the first player to hit two leadoff home runs in the same postseason?

5. Which Phillies pitcher was the first pitcher in 34 years to hit a World Series home run?
6. Who is the only Phillies reliever to have multiple wins in a World Series?

▶ 23

Here are several questions from the great postseason of 2008:

7. Who drew a crucial walk to spark a rally in the second game of the NLDS vs. Milwaukee?
8. Who hit two home runs in the series-clinching fourth game of the NLDS?
9. What was Cole Hamels' ERA in the NLDS?
10. His home run provided the winning margin in the first game of the NLCS vs. LA.
11. What personal tragedies did two members of the Phillies suffer on the day of the second game of the NLCS?
12. Whose two-run homer in the fourth game of the NLCS brought the Phillies back from a two-run deficit?
13. What veteran journeyman's pinch-hit, two-run homer won the fourth game of the NLCS?
14. Whom did Brad Lidge retire for the final out of the NLCS?
15. Who caught the final out of the NLCS?
16. What was the record of the Phillies at home during the 2008 postseason?
17. What item did Charlie Manuel place in each player's locker prior to Game 1 of the World Series vs. Tampa Bay?
18. Who was the Phillies' designated hitter in Game 1 of the World Series?
19. Which Phillie homered in Game 1 of the World Series?
20. Who was the winning pitcher in Game 1 of the World Series?
21. Who threw out the ceremonial first pitch in Game 3 of the World Series?
22. Game 3 holds what distinction in World Series history?
23. Who had the winning hit, and who scored the winning run in Game 3?
24. Who was the Phillies' starting pitcher in Game 3?
25. Which Phillies hit back-to-back home runs in Game 3?
26. What did country singer Tim McGraw scatter on the pitcher's mound prior to Game 3?

27. Name the Phillies who hit home runs in Game 4.
28. What distinction does Game 5 hold in World Series history?
29. How long did it take to complete Game 5?
30. Whose pinch-hit double led off the bottom of the sixth in Game 5?
31. Whose double set up the game and the series-winning run in Game 5?
32. Who drove in, and who scored, the series-winning run in Game 5?
33. Who was the winning pitcher in Game 5?
34. Whom did Brad Lidge strike out to record the final out of the 2008 WS?
35. Who was the Phillies' leading hitter in the 2008 WS?
36. How many people attended the 2008 championship parade?

▶ EXTRA BASE HIT

Who is the only Phillie to hit a pinch-hit home run in the World Series?

▶ WALK-OFF SINGLE

Who was the first Phillie to hit a walk-off single in the post-season?

ANSWERS

1. That is Shane Victorino, with 13 RBI in the 2008 postseason.
2. That's Cole Hamels, who went 4-0 in 2008.
3. That would be Brett Myers. Remember his 3–for–3 performance in the second game of the 2008 NLCS? He also drove in three runs that day.
4. Jimmy Rollins is the answer. In 2008, he opened the series-clinching fourth game of the NLDS with a home run, and also opened the series-clinching fifth game of the NLCS with a home run.
5. Joe Blanton was that pitcher. Blanton delivered a solo blast in Game 4 of the 2008 World Series. Not only was it the first homer of his career, it was the first extra base hit of his

career. He became the first pitcher since Oakland's Ken Holtzman in 1974 to hit a home run in a World Series game.

6. J.C. Romero had two victories in the 2008 World Series. No other Phillies reliever has ever had more than one victory in a World Series.

7. Brett Myers, who had a three-hit game in the NLCS vs. the Dodgers, worked a two-out walk off Brewers ace CC Sabathia. A couple of batters later, Shane Victorino hit the only postseason grand slam in Phillies history.

8. Pat Burrell hit two home runs in the decisive fourth game to put the game away, as the Phillies won the best-of-five series three games to one.

9. Hamels' ERA was 0.00 in the 2008 NLDS. He only pitched in the first game, tossing eight shutout innings.

10. Pat Burrell is the answer. The Phillies won the first game, 3-2. After a Chase Utley two-run homer tied the game at 2, Burrell delivered a solo shot to put the Phillies in front, and the 3-2 score held up.

11. Charlie Manuel's mother died, and Shane Victorino's grandmother died. Charlie learned of his mother's passing that morning. Victorino was told of his grandmother's death following the Phillies' Game 2 win. Charlie said the last time he spoke with his mother, she told him, "Charles Junior, you're going to win these games, you're going to go to the World Series." How right she was. The Phillies had a pair of angels in their outfield during that run to the World Series title.

12. Victorino crushed a liner that just cleared the right–field fence by inches.

13. His name is Matt Stairs, and his name will live in Phillies lore forever. Stairs was acquired by the Phillies on the last day of August as an extra left–handed bat off the bench. They were his 11th team in a 16-year big league career. With the game tied and Carlos Ruiz on base, Stairs took a mighty cut and deposited the ball deep into the left–field seats at Dodger Stadium. Stairs had hit 254 home runs in his career, but that was his first in the postseason, and by far the biggest of his life.

14. Lidge got the Dodgers' Nomar Garciaparra to pop out in foul territory for the final out of the series.

15. The pop-up was caught by catcher Carlos Ruiz. Usually, the player who secures the last out to win the pennant keeps the baseball, but Ruiz gave it to Lidge as a memento for all the games the closer had saved to get them to that point in the season.

16. It was 7-0. The Phillies didn't lose a single game at home in October.

17. Rubber ducks were given to the team to keep them loose, and to remind them to play relaxed and have fun. At one point during the season, Chase Utley remarked to Charlie Manuel that the manager was "as tight as a duck's ass," so the rubber duck symbolized loose and relaxed playing.

18. Backup catcher Chris Coste was the DH. Unfortunately, he went 0–for–4.

19. Second baseman Chase Utley, as the third batter of the game, drilled a two-run shot at Tropicana Field to give the Phillies an early 2-0 lead. The Phillies hung on to take Game 1 by a final of 3-2. Ironically, Utley tried to bunt earlier in the at-bat but bunted foul.

20. Cole Hamels was the pitcher. It was the last of his four victories in the 2008 postseason.

21. Hall of Famer Steve Carlton did the honors.

22. It was the latest-ending game in World Series history. Hampered by a 91–minute rain delay, Game 3 didn't begin until 10:06 p.m., and it ended at 1:47 a.m.

23. Carlos Ruiz's dribbler to third scored Eric Bruntlett to give the Phils a 5-4 win. Ruiz became the first player in World Series history to hit a walk-off infield single.

24. That was the ancient ex-Mariner, Jamie Moyer. In Game 3, the 45–year–old lefty made the first World Series start of his 22–year career. He went six and a third, gave up three runs, and finished with a no decision.

25. Chase Utley and Ryan Howard became the first Phillies duo to hit consecutive home runs in a World Series game.

26. Tim is the son of the late Phillies pitcher, Tug McGraw. He scattered Tug's ashes on the mound.

27. Ryan Howard, Joe Blanton, and Jayson Werth were the HR hitters. Howard hit two to join Lenny Dykstra as the only Phillies to have a multi-homer game in the World Series.

28. Game 5 was the first suspended game in World Series history. A cold, driving rain forced suspension of the game in the middle of the sixth inning, shortly after Tampa Bay had tied the score at 2.

29. Game 5 took two days, or roughly 49 hours and 28 minutes. The game began at 8:30 on Monday night, October 27th. It was halted at 11:10 p.m. Rain the next day continued its suspension. It finally resumed on Wednesday, October 29th at 8:40 p.m., the score tied at 2 in the bottom of the sixth. By 9:58 that night, the Phillies had their second World Championship.

30. That was reserve outfielder Geoff Jenkins. Two batters later, he scored to give the Phillies a 3-2 lead.

31. The answer is Pat Burrell. It was the left fielder's only hit of the Series. He was 0–for–13 coming into that at–bat, but in the seventh inning, he drove one off the top of the wall in deep center field to set up the winning run.

32. Third baseman Pedro Feliz had the game-winning hit. Eric Bruntlett, who pinch-ran for Burrell, scored the winning run. Feliz, signed as a free agent in the off-season, hit just .249 during the regular season, but sure came up huge in such a clutch situation.

33. Reliever J.C. Romero was the winning pitcher in the decisive Game 5. Hamels was the pitcher of record when Game 5 resumed, but when Ryan Madson gave up a seventh–inning homer to the Rays' Rocco Baldelli, Hamels was left with a no decision. Romero relieved Madson and tossed 14 pitches in one and a third to earn the victory. Romero was also the winning pitcher in Game 3.

34. Lidge whiffed Eric Hinske on three pitches, touching off the biggest celebration this town has ever seen. It was Lidge's seventh save of the postseason, which set an MLB record. He also capped a perfect season. Lidge, who saved 41 straight games in the regular season, went a perfect 48–for–48 in 2008!

35. The leading hitter was right fielder Jayson Werth, who hit .444.

36. City officials estimate that two million people attended the parade. Anyone who waded into that sea of humanity would've sworn there were more.

▶ EXTRA BASE HIT

That's Eric Bruntlett, who went deep in the Game 2 loss at Trop-icana Field.

▶ WALK-OFF SINGLE

That Phillie was Kim Batiste, whose single in the bottom of the 10th in the first game of the 1993 NLCS beat the Braves, 4-3.

19

Award-Winners

Many of baseball's most coveted awards have been won by Phillies. Many winners of baseball's most coveted awards have become Phillies. Many Phillies have gone on to win baseball's most coveted awards as members of other teams. Consider yourself an award-winner if you can correctly answer each of the questions in this section.

1. Who was the first Phillie to be voted National League MVP by the Baseball Writers Association of America?
2. Here's an easy one: Who was the only Phillie to win consecutive MVP awards?
3. Before Ryan Howard in 2008, who was the last Phillie to be runner-up in the MVP voting?
4. Who is the last Phillie to win the Cy Young Award?
5. Who is the last Phillie to win the NL batting title?
6. Which Phillie was the first relief pitcher to win an MVP award?
7. Who was the first National League player to win Rookie of the Year and MVP in consecutive seasons?
8. Which Phillie won Rookie of the Year in the National League, and later in his career became MVP in the American League?
9. Which Phillie was an AL Rookie of the Year, and while a Phillie, was MVP of the National League Championship Series?
10. Name the Phillies who have won the Cy Young Award.

More Award-Winning Trivia

11. Name the last Phillie to win the National League MVP award. (How's that for an easy question?)
12. Can you name the five former Phillies who won MVP awards?
13. Can you name the six former MVPs who played for the Phillies?
14. There are four former Cy Young Award-winners who played for the Phillies. Can you name them?
15. There are three former Phillies who have won the Cy Young Award. Can you name them?
16. Seven former Rookies of the Year have played for the Phillies. Who are they?
17. Who was the first Phillie to be named NL Rookie of the Year?
18. Can you name the four Phillies who have won Rookie of the Year honors as voted by the Baseball Writers Association of America?
19. Which Phillie won the National League batting title while playing for two teams in the same season?
20. Who is the only Phillies catcher to win a Silver Slugger award?
21. What three ex-Phillies players have gone on to win Manager of the Year as voted by the Baseball Writers Association of America?
22. What two Phillies broadcasters have been presented with the Ford C. Frick Award?
23. Who is the Phillies' only two-time batting champ? (This answer was revealed in an earlier section.)
24. Who was the first Phillie to win a Gold Glove award?
25. Who was the last Phillies outfielder to win a Gold Glove?

▶ EXTRA BASE HIT

While we're on the subject of Gold Gloves, who was the last Phillies pitcher to win one?

▶ WALK-OFF SINGLE

How about the last Phillies catcher to win a Gold Glove?

ANSWERS

1. Chuck Klein was the first Phillie to earn Most Valuable Player honors. Klein won the award in 1932, after batting .348 with 38 HRs and 137 RBI. His 38 homers led the league. He also had an NL-leading 226 hits. Thanks to Chuck, the Phils finished in fourth place, which was their highest finish in 15 years.

2. That, of course, was Mike Schmidt, who was league MVP in 1980 and 1981.

3. It was Lenny Dykstra, who finished second in the National League MVP voting in 1993. In 2008, Howard finished second to Albert Pujols of St. Louis.

4. That would be Steve Bedrosian. "Bedrock" won the Cy Young in 1987, when he had 40 saves and a 2.83 ERA.

5. It's been a long time since a Phillie had the league's highest batting average. Richie Ashburn is the last Phillie to do it. Ashburn was the NL batting champ in 1958 with a .350 average.

6. He was one of the heroes of 1950, Jim Konstanty. His 16-7 record with 22 saves and a 2.66 ERA not only propelled the "Whiz Kids" to the World Series, it also won him the MVP award. Konstanty edged Stan Musial in the balloting by 128 points to become the first reliever in baseball history to win an MVP award.

7. Who else but Ryan Howard. In 2006, Howard was called up for good on July 1st. He went on to hit 22 homers and was voted Rookie of the Year. The following season, his first full season in the majors, Howard had one for the ages: .313, 58 HRs, and 149 RBI. His HR and RBI totals led the league and enabled Ryan to outdistance Albert Pujols in the MVP voting. Ryan was the first player since Cal Ripken in 1983 to win Rookie of the Year and MVP in back-to-back seasons.

8. That's Dick Allen. As a Phillie in 1964, when he was called Richie, Allen won NL Rookie of the Year. In 1972, while playing for the White Sox and known as Dick, he was the American League MVP. Allen led the AL in homers and RBI, while hitting .308.

9. His name is Gary Matthews. He was NL Rookie of the Year in 1973 as a San Francisco Giant. Ten years later, he was the MVP of the NLCS after hitting .429 with three homers and eight RBI to lead the Phillies past the Dodgers and into the World Series.

10. There are three Cy Young winners: Steve Carlton, John Denny, and Steve Bedrosian. Carlton, as you know, has won it four times ('72, '77, '80, and '82), the only multiple winner from the Phillies. Denny won it in '83, after going 19-6 with a 2.37 ERA.

11. It is the man they call J-Roll, Jimmy Rollins. The Phillies shortstop had his best season in 2007 when he led the Phillies to the NL East title. Rollins batted .296 with 30 homers, 94 RBI, and 212 hits. He also stole 41 bases, had 38 doubles, and 20 triples. Rollins led the league with 139 runs, and set a major league record with 716 at-bats. He is the first player in ML history with 200 hits, 15 triples, 25 HRs and 25 steals in the same season. He also became just the second Phillie to reach the 30/30 club. That is called doing it all. And that is why Rollins was voted the league's MVP in 2007.

12. Pitcher Bucky Walters, first baseman Dolph Camilli, first baseman Dick Allen, pitcher Willie Hernandez, and second baseman Ryne Sandberg are the ex-Phillies who've won the MVP award elsewhere. Walters was traded by the Phils to the Reds in 1938. In '39, he went 27-11 to win MVP. Camilli was traded to the Dodgers in '38 after just three seasons with the Phillies. By '41, he was MVP, leading the league in homers and RBI. You know about Allen, who won MVP honors in the American League with the White Sox in '72. The year 1984 was a particularly difficult one for Phillies fans. They watched two former players sweep the award that year. Sandberg, who left the Phils in the worst trade since Dolph Camilli, became the National League MVP with the Cubs, while Hernandez, traded to Detroit in March of '84, won it in the AL.

13. The former MVPs who became Phillies are, in chronological order: Jimmie Foxx, Bobby Shantz, Dick Groat, Pete Rose, Joe Morgan, and Dale Murphy. Foxx played for the Phils in 1945, and was MVP in '32, '33, and '38 with the A's. Shantz played for the Phils in '64, and was MVP in '52, also with the A's. Groat, MVP in '60 with Pittsburgh, played with the Phils in

'66 and '67. Rose was MVP with the Reds in '73, and played for the Phillies from '79 to '83. Morgan was MVP in both '75 and '76, and was a Phillie in '83. Murphy also won MVP in back-to-back years, '82 and '83, and then played for the Phillies from '90 to '92.

14. They are Jim Lonborg, Sparky Lyle, Fernando Valenzuela, and Mark Davis. Lonborg won the Cy Young in 1967 with Boston, then joined the Phillies in 1973 and pitched for the club until '79. Lyle won it with the Yankees in '77 and later played for the Phils from '80 to '82. Valenzuela was the NL Cy Young winner in '81, and was a Phillie in '94. Davis won it with San Diego in '89 after notching 44 saves. He joined the Phillies in '93.

15. The three pitchers who left Philadelphia and went on to win Cy Young Awards are: Ferguson Jenkins, Willie Hernandez, and Mark Davis. In one of the worst deals in Phillies history, Jenkins was traded after pitching just eight games in his career. Not only did he win the Cy Young with the Cubs in 1971, but 20 years later he'd get elected to the Hall of Fame. Hernandez, in another awful trade, went to Detroit in March of '84 and won the award that season. As for Davis, he's on both lists because he actually started his career with the Phils. He was their number–one pick in 1979, made his ML debut with them in 1980, and also pitched in 9 games in '81. In '82, he was part of the deal with San Francisco that landed Joe Morgan and Al Holland. Davis was traded back to the Phillies by the Braves in '93. In between, he became a Cy Young Award-winner.

16. They are Roy Sievers (ROY in 1949, Phillie: 1962-64), Pete Rose (ROY: '63, Phillie: '79-'83), Stan Bahnsen (ROY: '68, Phillie: '82), Ted Sizemore (ROY: '69, Phillie: '77-'78), Gary Matthews (ROY: '73, Phillie: '81-'83), Fernando Valenzuela (ROY: '81, Phillie: '94), and Benito Santiago (ROY: '87, Phillie: '96).

17. Pitcher Jack Sanford was voted National League Rookie of the Year by the Baseball Writers Association of America in 1957. Sanford went 19-8 with 15 complete games that season. But in yet another horrendous move by the Phillies, he was traded to the Giants in 1959. Sanford had his best season in 1962, going 24-7 and finishing as the runner-up in the Cy Young voting.

18. I spotted you the first one, so you know Sanford. Then there's Richie Allen (1964), Scott Rolen (1997), and Ryan Howard (2005).

19. Harry Walker, "Harry the Hat," led the league in 1947 with a .363 average. He started the season with St. Louis, and in 10 games he went 5–for–25. Traded to the Phils on May 3rd for Ron Northey, Walker went on to bat .371 in 130 games. The Phillies shipped him to Chicago following the '48 season.

20. It was Darren Daulton, in 1992. Daulton hit .270 that season with 27 homers and won Silver Slugger honors. That season was also memorable for "Dutch" because his 109 RBI led the National League. He joined Roy Campanella, Johnny Bench, and Gary Carter as the only catchers ever to lead the National League in runs batted in.

21. Again, I spotted you one in a previous section. Larry Bowa was the only Phillies skipper to win the award. But the other two aren't as easy. That's because most people don't realize that George "Sparky" Anderson once played for the Phillies. Sparky was the Manager of the Year in the American League in 1984 while piloting the Tigers to the World Championship. He played second base for the Phillies in 1959, and batted .218 in 152 games (his only season in the big leagues). The other ex-Phillie to win Manager of the Year also won it in the AL. He is Davey Johnson, who was an infielder for the Phillies in '77 and '78. Johnson played in 122 games and hit .273. Interestingly, in '78, he hit two pinch-hit grand slams. Johnson was AL Manager of the Year with Baltimore in 1997. The award has only been given by the Baseball Writers Association since 1983.

22. The two broadcasters are By Saam and Harry Kalas. Saam received the award in 1990, and Kalas in 2002. The Frick Award is named for the former National League president and its winners are honored in an exhibit at the National Baseball Hall of Fame.

23. It's the man who patrolled center field in the 1950s, and later graced the broadcast booth for so many years: none other than Richie Ashburn. "Whitey" led the NL in 1955 with a .338 average. He won the batting title again in 1958 when he hit .350. This was a clue in the second "Who Am I?" puzzle in Section 11.

24. That was Bobby Wine. The Phillies shortstop won a Gold
Glove in 1963, the first Phillie ever to be so honored.

25. Shane Victorino won in 2008. Victorino made it two years in a
row that a Phillies center fielder took Gold Glove honors.
Aaron Rowand won the award in 2007.

▶ EXTRA BASE HIT

The last Phils pitcher to win a Gold Glove award was Steve Carlton in 1981.

▶ WALK-OFF SINGLE

Would you believe it's Mike Lieberthal? "Liebie" won a Gold
Glove award in 1999.

20

Weird, Wild Stuff

For a team that's been around as long as the Phillies, there's bound to be some weird, wild stuff that's gone on. The Phillies have had more than their share. Weird occurrences, wild facts, the bizarre and the off the wall, it's all encapsulated in this section. We'll also wade through the miscellaneous minutiae. See how well-versed you are in the weird, wild stuff that pertains to the Phillies.

1. Name the Phillies pitcher whose final major league win was a no-hitter? (Hint: He pitched the no-no before joining the Phillies.)
2. What was the nickname the Phillies tried to change their name to in 1944?
3. Why was Curt Simmons forced to miss the 1950 pennant race and World Series?
4. Which Eagles head coach once played for the Phillies?
5. Who is the youngest player in Phillies history?
6. Who is the oldest player in Phillies history?
7. After retiring from the game, which Phillies player became a sportswriter for the *Philadelphia Inquirer*?
8. Which Phillie was the first major league player drafted in World War II?
9. Who was the original Phillie Phanatic?
10. What Phillie was shot by a crazed female fan, later becoming the inspiration for the novel and movie, *The Natural*?

More Weird, Wild Stuff

11. Which Phillie is the oldest player to lead the National League in hits in a season?
12. Who is the only Phillies pitcher to start on Opening Day, and close the season finale in the same year?
13. Who is the only Phillie to be part of the '50, '80, '83, and '93 pennant-winners?
14. Who was Alice Roth and what happened to her at a 1957 Phillies game?
15. Who is the only Phillie to play all nine positions?
16. Who is the only non-pitcher to earn a pitching victory for the Phillies?
17. Who is the last non-pitcher to pitch for the Phils?
18. Who is the tallest player in Phillies franchise history?
19. Which Phillies pitcher holds the major league record for highest percentage of a team's total wins in a single season?
20. Name the high–wire performer who tightrope–walked across the top of Veterans Stadium.

Another Trip Around the Bases with the Weird and Wild

21. Who was the Phillies' first African-American player?
22. Who was the first African-American pitcher to appear in a regular season game for the Phillies?
23. Who was the first Latin American–born player in Phillies history?
24. Who was the first Japanese–born player in Phillies history?
25. Who was the last University of Pennsylvania alumnus to play for the Phillies?
26. What Phillie was once traded for himself?
27. Which player spent the most seasons as a Phillie?
28. Which Phillie was the first player in major league history to have a perfect 1,000 fielding percentage for a season?
29. Who is the only Phillie to have a 200-hit season during the decade of the 1990s?
30. Name the Phillies pitcher who was born with six fingers on each hand.

Still Another Trip Around the Bases with the Weird and Wild

31. Which Phillie got into a fight with teammate Dick Allen in 1965?
32. What is the largest Opening Day crowd in Philadelphia baseball history?
33. What is the highest uniform number ever worn by a Phillie?
34. What is the lowest uniform number ever worn by a Phillie?
35. Name the Phillie who is the only player in major league history with a World Series championship ring and an NBA championship ring.
36. True or false—the Phillies once had a female scout.
37. True or false—the Phillies once had a player named Phillie.
38. Which Phillie went on to a career with the CIA?
39. Which Phillie went on to a career as an evangelist?
40. Which Phillie went on to become president of the National League?
41. Which Phillie once punched an umpire during a game, and then later went on to become an umpire himself?
42. Name the last brother combination to play for the Phillies.
43. Name the third–generation big leaguer to play for the Phillies.
44. Name the only two Hall of Famers to serve as Phillies coaches.
45. Who was the Phillie who plunged to his death after being swept over Niagara Falls?

▶ EXTRA BASE HIT

What historic milestone in Phillies history occurred on July 15, 2007?

ANSWERS

1. This may be my favorite question. There is a onetime Phillie who pitched a no-hitter, and never won another big league game again. His name is Joe Cowley. As a White

Sox player, he no-hit the California Angels on September 19, 1986. Cowley walked seven in the game, and actually gave up a run on a sacrifice fly. But no hits. He struck out eight, including Jayson Werth's uncle, Dick Schofield. In his next three starts for the Angels, Cowley had a loss, a no-decision, and another loss. He was then dealt to the Phillies for outfielder Gary Redus. The right-hander pitched in five games as a Phillie in 1987, and went 0-4. He never pitched in the bigs again.

2. It was the Blue Jays. Bob Carpenter thought a new name would change the culture of his losing franchise, so in 1944, he held a contest to rename the team. Blue Jays was the winner. But the new name was never officially changed, and the fans and media still referred to the team as the "Phillies." By 1949, Carpenter scrapped the idea, and the alternate nickname became a footnote in history.

3. Simmons' National Guard unit was called into active duty in September of that year. He missed a month of the season, which denied him a chance to win 20 games. Because of the layoff, he was also kept off the World Series roster. This was during the Korean War, and Simmons would also spend all of 1951 in the service.

4. That was Pro Football Hall of Famer Earle "Greasy" Neale. "Greasy" was an outfielder on the 1921 team, batting .211 in 22 games. He had much greater success as a football coach, guiding the Eagles to NFL titles in 1948 and 1949.

5. Ralph "Putsy" Caballero, an infielder, was 16 years old when called up to the Phillies in 1944. This was during World War II when players were scarce. "Putsy" appeared in four games that season, going 0-for-4 at the plate. He'd spend his entire eight-year career with the Phils and hit .228 in 322 career games.

6. That would be Kaiser Wilhelm, who was 47 years old. The right-handed pitcher came out of retirement in 1921 to appear in four games for the Phillies. He pitched eight innings, gave up three runs and 11 hits, and his record was 0-0.

7. His name was Stan Baumgartner, and he was a member of the 1915 pennant-winners. He later became the Phillies beat writer for the *Inquirer*, and covered the 1950 pennant-winners. Baumgartner was a pitcher during an eight-season big league career spent with both the Phillies and the

Philadelphia Athletics. His career numbers were 26-21 with a 3.70 ERA.

8. Hugh Mulcahy holds the distinction of being the first player drafted for service in WWII. He missed almost four full seasons as a result. Mulcahy also holds the distinction of never having had a winning season in nine years in the majors—which, no doubt, was how he earned his nickname. Hugh was known as "Losing Pitcher" Mulcahy. "Losing Pitcher" twice led the league in losses. In fact, in 1940, he lost 12 in a row and yet made the All-Star team. He also had 21 complete games that season, while finishing with a 13-22 record.

9. Dave Raymond was the first man to wear the green suit. Raymond, a former front office intern, portrayed the Phanatic from its debut in 1978 until 1993. In 16 years, he missed just eight games. His father, Tubby Raymond, was a legendary football coach at the University of Delaware, and is enshrined in the College Football Hall of Fame.

10. Eddie Waitkus was the victim. On June 15, 1949, in Chicago, Waitkus received a message from a young woman named Ruth Ann Steinhagen. Eddie didn't know her, but she claimed to be from his hometown, that she had something important to tell him, and that it was urgent that they meet. When Waitkus arrived at her hotel room that night, Steinhagen took out a rifle and shot him in the chest. While the Phillies first baseman survived, he was seriously wounded, eventually undergoing five surgeries. Eddie rehabbed hard during the winter, and made a complete recovery. He returned to the starting lineup for the 1950 season, playing a key role for the Whiz Kids.

11. That's Pete Rose. He led the league at age 40 with 140 hits in 1981.

12. It was Brett Myers, in a very unusual situation for the Phillies in 2007. Myers started the opener that season vs. Atlanta, but was not involved in the decision. Following his third start, Myers was moved to the bullpen and became the team's closer. He finished with 21 saves in 48 relief appearances, including the NL East clincher over Washington. Myers struck out Washington's Wily Mo Peña to end the ballgame, as the Phillies earned their first playoff berth in 14 years. Myers got

the first out and the last out of the 2007 season, both by strikeout.

13. It could only be Richie Ashburn. The iconic "Whitey" was, of course, the center fielder on the 1950 team. Ashburn moved to the broadcast booth after his playing days, and called the action for the 1980, 1983, and 1993 teams, all of which reached the World Series.

14. Alice Roth was a fan who was once struck by two foul balls in the same game, both off the bat of Richie Ashburn. It happened in 1957. Ashburn sent a line drive foul into the stands, striking Mrs. Roth. As she was being taken away on a stretcher, Ashburn drilled her a second time.

15. The answer is Cookie Rojas. A utility infielder by trade, Rojas even pitched once in a 1967 game. That mound appearance meant he'd spent time at all nine positions in his career as a Phillie.

16. Believe it or not, it's slugging first baseman Jimmie Foxx. The Hall of Famer actually pitched in nine games in 1945, starting two. He went 1–0 that year with a 1.59 ERA in $22^2/_3$ innings.

17. That would be infielder Tomas Perez in 2002. He pitched a third of an inning that season, gave up no runs, with no hits, and had no walks or strikeouts.

18. That's six–foot eight–inch Gene Conley, the pro hoops player.

19. Who else but Steve Carlton. Carlton earned 27 of the Phillies' 59 victories in 1972; that's a phenomenal 46 percent. Amazing.

20. Who can forget the great Karl Wallenda? He did it twice: once in 1972, and again in 1976.

21. John Kennedy was the first African–American player. An infielder, Kennedy went to spring training with the club in 1957, 10 full years after Jackie Robinson became a Dodger. He appeared in five regular season games that year as a defensive replacement. Kennedy batted only twice, going 0–for–2, and by May was sent down to the minors. He never played in the majors again.

22. His name is Hank Mason, and he pitched five innings in relief in a game in 1958, the first African American to pitch for the Phillies. He was back with the Phillies in 1960, making three relief appearances.

23. Chili Gomez, who joined the Phillies in 1935. A native of Mexico, the middle infielder played two seasons for the Phillies. In '36, he was the starting second baseman, batting .232 in 108 games.

24. Tadahito Iguchi, who joined the Phillies in 2007. Iguchi came to the Phils on July 28th from the Chicago White Sox. He hit .304 in 45 games and played a crucial role filling in for an injured Chase Utley. It's doubtful the Phillies would've won the NL East without the contribution of their first Japanese–born player.

25. Doug Glanville, Penn Class of '91, played center field for the Phillies from 1998 to 2002, and 2004.

26. That was Vic Power. In September 1964, the Phillies agreed to send pitcher Marcelino Lopez, and a player to be named later, to the L.A. Angels for Vic Power. The player to be named later became Power, who was sent back to the Angels at the end of the season to complete the deal.

27. It was Mike Schmidt, who spent 18 seasons in Phillies pinstripes.

28. It was Danny Litwhiler, who accomplished the feat in 1942. Litwhiler played left field for the '42 Phils. In 151 games, he fielded 317 chances without making an error, a first in major league history. Following his playing days, Litwhiler went on to a successful career as a college baseball coach, spending 20 years at Michigan State, where he coached future big league stars Kirk Gibson and Steve Garvey. Litwhiler also invented the radar gun, used to measure the speed of pitches.

29. If you said Len Dykstra, you'd be wrong. Dykstra twice had over 190, but never 200. That distinction goes to Doug Glanville. The Penn Quaker had 204 hits in 1999. It was a career year for Glanville, who batted .325 that season.

30. That's Antonio Alfonseca, and he pitched for the Phillies in 2007. Alfonseca was born in La Romana in the Dominican Republic in 1972 with an extra finger on each hand and an extra toe on each foot. When he played for the Florida Marlins his teammates nicknamed him "El Pulpo," which is Spanish for "the octopus." In '07, Alfonseca went 5-2, with a 5.44 ERA and eight saves in 61 games for the NL East champion Phillies. At six feet, five inches and throwing in the high 90s, he could've been twice the pitcher Mordecai "Three-Finger" Brown was!

31. That was first baseman/outfielder Frank Thomas. He and Allen got into it during batting practice before a game in '65. As a result, the Phillies released Thomas after the game.
32. The home opener in 1993. A crowd of 60,985 showed up that day at the Vet. The Phillies opened the season that year by sweeping three games in Houston, and then returned home to Philadelphia, where 60,985 fans welcomed them. Despite a two–homer, five–RBI effort from Darren Daulton, the Phillies lost to the Cubs, 11-7.
33. Number 99 has been worn by three different Phillies: Mitch Williams (1993), Turk Wendell (2001), and So Taguchi (2008).
34. Numbers 0 and 00: 0 was worn by Al Oliver (1984) and 00 was worn by Omar Olivares (1995) and Rick White (2006).
35. That's pitcher Gene Conley, who also played pro basketball. Conley won a World Series ring with the 1957 Milwaukee Braves, and was a member of the NBA champion Boston Celtics in 1959.
36. It's true. Her name is Edith Houghton and she worked for the club as a scout in 1946.
37. That's also true, although he spelled his name with a "y" instead of "ie." Dave Philley played for the Phillies from 1958 to 1960. Philley was a switch-hitter who played the outfield and first base for the Phils, batting .300 in 204 games. He also played a couple of years with the Philadelphia A's in an 18-year, big league career. Philley was a lifetime .270 hitter.
38. His name is Pete Sivess, and he pitched for the Phillies from 1936 to 1938. Sivess was a naval officer during World War II. In 1948, he joined a newly formed little government organization called the Central Intelligence Agency (you've probably heard of it). Sivess' career with the CIA spanned 25 years.
39. He was the aptly named Billy Sunday. After retiring from baseball, Sunday became an evangelist. What could be more appropriate? Sunday was a pitcher/outfielder for the 1890 Phillies.
40. That would be Bill White. White played first base for the Phillies from 1966 to 1968. In 1989, he succeeded A. Bartlett Giamatti as NL president and served in that role until 1994. White also spent 18 years as a broadcaster, mostly with the New York Yankees.

41. It was the hot-tempered Sherry Magee. In a game in 1911, after striking out, Magee punched the home plate umpire in the mouth. The Phillies outfielder was fined and suspended. After his playing days, Magee, in the irony of all ironies, became an umpire. He umped in the New York–Penn league in 1927, then joined the National League as an umpire in 1928.
42. Dave and Dennis Bennett were the last pair of brothers to play together for the Phillies. They were pitchers on the 1964 team.
43. That's David Bell. His dad, Buddy Bell, a third baseman, was a five-time All-Star who played 18 seasons in the majors, mostly with Texas. His grandfather, Gus Bell, was an outfielder who spent 15 seasons in the majors, mostly with Cincinnati. Gus was a four-time All-Star. David played third for the Phils from 2003 to 2006 in a 12-year big league career. There is one other Phillie who is sort of a third–generation guy. Jayson Werth's grandfather, Ducky Schofield, played 19 years in the majors. His stepfather, Dennis Werth, played three big league seasons. But Dennis is Jayson's stepfather, not his biological father.
44. They are Chuck Klein and Bob Lemon. Klein, the great slugger from the 1930s who was enshrined in the Hall in 1980, coached the Phillies from 1942 to 1945. Lemon, a seven-time, 20-game winner with Cleveland, made it to Cooperstown in 1976. Lemon was on the Phillies coaching staff in 1961—not a good year to be with the Phillies. They lost 107, including that record streak of 23 straight.
45. It was the legendary Ed Delahanty, who died on July 2, 1903. He was playing for Washington at the time, but had been suspended from the team while the Senators were playing a series in Detroit. On the train ride home, Delahanty reportedly became so drunk he was threatening other passengers, and caused such a disturbance that the conductor kicked him off the train near the International Bridge in Fort Erie, Ontario. According to a *New York Times* report from July 8, 1903, Delahanty started to walk toward the American side of the bridge when the bridge's night watchman ordered Delahanty back to shore. Delahanty ignored him. What the future Hall of Famer didn't realize was that the drawbridge was open to

allow a boat to pass. It's believed that he fell through the opening and plunged into the Niagara River. But all these many decades later mystery still surrounds the death of Ed Delahanty. Did he really fall, or was he pushed? Might he have jumped? Those questions remain unanswered to this day.

▶ EXTRA BASE HIT

July 15, 2007 was the day the Phillies suffered the franchise's 10,000th loss. The Cardinals beat the Phillies that night, 10-2, for loss number 10,000.

21

The Ballparks

The Phillies' on-field history has been written in five primary ballparks. It all started in 1883, when the new franchise played at Recreation Park. In 1887, they moved to what was later called Baker Bowl. By 1938, the club joined the Philadelphia Athletics at Shibe Park, which would one day be renamed Connie Mack Stadium. They were the sole occupants of Connie Mack following the Athletics' move to Kansas City in 1954. Connie Mack Stadium was the Phillies' home through the 1970 season. In 1971, they took up residency in cutting-edge, state-of-the-art Veterans Stadium. The infamous Vet, known for its unforgiving turf and rowdy fans, was the site where the team clinched its first World Series title. After 32 years at the Vet, the Phillies moved to their current "field of dreams," beautiful Citizens Bank Park. In this section, we highlight the trivia surrounding the Phillies' home fields.

1. Who scored the final run at Connie Mack Stadium?
2. In 1956, the Phillies replaced the scoreboard at Shibe Park with a newer one that was formerly used at what American League stadium?
3. Whose 14th-inning home run beat the Phillies at Shibe Park on the last day of the 1951 season, helping his team earn a tie with the Giants for the National League pennant?
4. Who had the final hit at Connie Mack Stadium?
5. Who was the winning pitcher in the final game at Connie Mack Stadium?

6. Another "final" from Connie Mack: Who hit the final home run?
7. And another: Who hit the Phillies' final home run?
8. For whom was Shibe Park named?
9. Which Phillie had the most home runs at Shibe Park/Connie Mack Stadium?
10. Prior to 1968, what was the distance to the center–field fence at Connie Mack Stadium?

More Ballpark Trivia

11. For how many innings did the longest Phillies game played at Shibe Park last?
12. Where in Philadelphia was Shibe Park/Connie Mack Stadium located, and what now occupies that site?
13. What was the largest crowd in Shibe Park history?
14. In what year was Shibe Park renamed Connie Mack Stadium?

Now for Some Veterans Stadium Firsts

15. How was the first ball delivered on Opening Day, 1971, at Veterans Stadium?
16. Who had the first hit at the Vet?
17. Who hit the Vet's first home run?
18. Who was the first batter in Veterans Stadium history?
19. What pitcher earned the first win at the Vet?
20. Who scored the first run at the Vet?

More About the Vet

21. What was the Phillies' starting battery for the first game at the Vet?

22. What former Phillie was Montreal's starting shortstop in the first game at the Vet?
23. Who was the home plate umpire in the first game at the Vet?
24. Who had the most pitching victories in the history of the Vet?
25. Who hit the longest home run in the history of the Vet?
26. Who played in the most games at the Vet?
27. Who is the only man to hit the "Liberty Bell" that once hung from the fourth level in center field at the Vet?
28. Now for some Veterans Stadium "lasts," beginning with this: Who won the last game at the Vet?
29. Who was the winning pitcher in the final game at the Vet?
30. Who hit the final home run at the Vet?

Still More from the Ballparks

31. Who hit the most home runs at the Vet?
32. Who delivered the final hit at the Vet?
33. Who made the final out?
34. Who scored the final run?
35. Who was the home plate umpire in the final game at the Vet?
36. Now to the "Bank": On what date was the first regular season game played at Citizens Bank Park?
37. Who was the Phillies' starting pitcher in the first game at Citizens Bank Park?
38. Who had the first hit?
39. Who had the first home run?
40. Who was the first Phillies pitcher to record a victory at Citizens Bank Park?
41. Who had the first stolen base?

More About the "Bank"

42. Who hit the first "walk-off" home run?
43. Who hit the first grand slam at Citizens Bank Park?
44. Who hit the first grand slam by a Phillie?
45. Who had the first inside-the-park home run at Citizens Bank Park?

46. Who had the first four-hit game at Citizens Bank Park?
47. Who hit the longest home run at Citizens Bank Park?
48. What is the distance to the deepest part of Citizens Bank Park?
49. What happens when a Phillie hits a home run at Citizens Bank Park?
50. Which four Phillies greats are immortalized with statues at Citizens Bank Park?
51. What is the bullpen configuration at Citizens Bank Park?

Rounding Third at the Ballparks

52. Let's turn back the clock to the days of Baker Bowl: Where in Philadelphia was Baker Bowl located?
53. For whom was Baker Bowl named?
54. What was the distance down the right–field line at Baker Bowl?
55. What was used at one time to trim the infield and outfield grass at Baker Bowl?
56. The clubhouse at Baker Bowl was in center field, with windows that faced the playing field…Can you name the player who once hit a ball through one of those clubhouse windows?
57. Which storied slugger played the final game of his illustrious career at Baker Bowl?
58. What tragedy occurred at Baker Bowl in 1903?
59. In the 1930s, how many feet high was Baker Bowl's right–field fence?
60. What product was advertised for many years on a huge sign on the right–field fence?
61. When was the last Phillies game played at Baker Bowl?

► EXTRA BASE HIT

On what date was Veterans Stadium demolished?

ANSWERS   1. Phillies catcher Tim McCarver scored the
winning run in the 10th inning to give the
Phillies a 2-1 victory over Montreal in the
final game at Connie Mack Stadium.

2. Its former home was Yankee Stadium.

3. Hall of Famer Jackie Robinson's home run set up the historic
playoff between the Brooklyn Dodgers and the New York
Giants. It was decided by Bobby Thomson's "shot heard
'round the world" as the Giants won the pennant.

4. Oscar Gamble of the Phillies, whose walk-off single drove in
McCarver in the 10th to win it in the stadium's swan song.

5. Reliever Dick Selma pitched one and two–thirds innings and
retired all five batters he faced to earn the victory.

6. The final home run at Connie Mack Stadium was hit by
Montreal's John Bateman. The Expos' catcher, who later
became a Phillie, hit a two-run shot in the ninth inning of a
10-3 Expos win on September 29, 1970, the third to last game
in the ballpark's history.

7. Phillies third baseman Don Money hit a solo shot in the sixth
inning of a 5-3 win over the Cubs on September 25, 1970.
Money's homer followed a solo drive by Tim McCarver as the
Phils went back-to-back off the Cubs' Phil Regan. They would
go homerless in the final five games at Connie Mack Stadium.

8. Shibe Park was named for Benjamin F. Shibe, owner of the
A's.

9. Del Ennis went deep a record 133 times at Shibe/Connie
Mack.

10. It was a whopping 447 feet! The Phillies decreased the
distance in 1968 to 410.

11. It was an amazing 19 innings for an 8-7 win over the Reds on
September 15, 1950.

12. North 21st and Lehigh Avenue in North Philadelphia, a
location now occupied by Deliverance Evangelistic Church.

13. A crowd of 41,660 turned out on April 11, 1947 to see
Brooklyn's Jackie Robinson play his first game in
Philadelphia. They also saw the Phillies sweep a
doubleheader.

14. In 1953, Connie Mack Stadium was born.
15. The ball was dropped from a helicopter that hovered above the field and into the waiting mitt of catcher Mike Ryan, just before the home opener against the Montreal Expos.
16. Phillies shortstop Larry Bowa batted lead-off for the Phillies, and opened the home half of the first inning with a single.
17. The same guy who had the last home run at Connie Mack also had the first HR at the Vet. It was Don Money. He led off the sixth inning with a solo shot that tied the game at 1.
18. That was Montreal outfielder Boots Day. He batted lead-off for the Expos and grounded out to Phillies first baseman Deron Johnson. So, Boots also made the first out in Veterans Stadium history.
19. Hall of Famer Jim Bunning went seven and a third and gave up one earned run in beating the Expos, 4-1, in the first game at the Vet.
20. Expos second baseman Ron Hunt scored on a sixth–inning double by Bob Bailey.
21. Bunning was the starting pitcher; McCarver was the starting catcher.
22. That was Bobby Wine, who played for the Phillies from 1960 to 1968, winning the franchise's first Gold Glove.
23. Philadelphia native Shag Crawford was behind the plate for the Vet's opener.
24. It could only be Steve Carlton, who won 138 games at Broad and Pattison.
25. Pirates great Willie Stargell unloaded a Jim Bunning pitch into section 601 on June 25, 1971. It was a solo blast, the longest in the stadium's history. To commemorate the home run, a yellow star with a black "S" was painted on the seat where it landed.
26. It was Mike Schmidt, with 1,202 games. He played in more games than any other Phillie. He played more seasons than any other Phillie, and the Vet was his home park for his entire 18-year career. Andre Dawson played more games there than any other opponent.
27. That man is Greg "The Bull" Luzinski. Bull clanged the "Bell" with a solo homer on May 16, 1972. It was the Phillies' only run in an 8-1 loss to the Cubs. Luzinski led the Phillies that year with 18 home runs.

28. That would be those Atlanta Braves. In the midst of yet another NL East title, the Braves beat the Phillies, 5-2, on September 28, 2003. It was their 101st win of the season.

29. It was Greg Maddux, the four-time Cy Young Award winner. Maddux went five innings, surrendering two earned runs to finish 16-11 that season.

30. The final homer was by Jim Thome. It came on September 27, 2003, the penultimate game at the Vet. Thome hit it with two out in the eighth inning vs. the Braves. It was his second homer of the game and his 47th of the season, which at the time was one off the Phillies' single-season record.

31. Who else but Mike Schmidt. The iconic Phillies slugger belted 265 of his 548 career home runs at Veterans Stadium.

32. Pat Burrell hit a one-out single in the bottom of the ninth in the final game at the Vet.

33. Chase Utley followed Burrell's ninth–inning single by hitting into a 5-4-3 double-play. And with that, the Veterans Stadium era came to a close.

34. Braves outfielder Andruw Jones scored on a fifth–inning double by Robert Fick, the final run ever scored at Veterans Stadium.

35. Philadelphia native Jerry Crawford called the balls and strikes in the final game at the Vet. Jerry is the son of Shag Crawford, the man who was the home plate umpire for the Vet's inaugural game.

36. The Citizens Bank Park era officially got under way on April 12, 2004, vs. the Cincinnati Reds. The Phillies lost the park's opener, 4-1, on a cold and rainy afternoon.

37. Left–hander Randy Wolf was the starting, and losing, pitcher in the Phillies' 4-1 loss.

38. The first batter got the first hit. Reds second baseman D'Angelo Jimenez led off with a ground–rule double to christen the new ballpark.

39. Phillies right–fielder Bobby Abreu drilled a solo shot in the bottom of the first. It was also the Phillies' first hit, and first run, in their new home.

40. Left–handed reliever Rheal Cormier earned the first win by a Phillies pitcher. Cormier was the winning pitcher vs. the Reds on April 15, 2004, the second game ever played at Citizens Bank Park. Cormier pitched a scoreless eighth inning before

the Phillies scored four in their half of the inning to win it 6-4, the first Phillies win at the "Bank."

41. Marlon Byrd swiped the first base at Citizens Bank Park. The center fielder stole second after drawing a one-out walk in the third inning of the ballpark's inaugural game.

42. Doug Glanville, of all people, hit the first "walk-off" HR in Citizens Bank Park history on April 18, 2004. The center fielder gave the Phillies a 5-4 victory over Montreal with a lead-off homer in the bottom of the ninth. It was the first of Glanville's two home runs that season.

43. The Braves' Andruw Jones hit the grand slam off Kevin Millwood on May 27, 2004, the 21st game in the ballpark's history.

44. The first grand slam by a Phillie was hit by Marlon Byrd. It came in the seventh inning of a 10-0 win over Milwaukee on August 29, 2004.

45. None other than Jimmy Rollins. The Phillies speedster touched 'em all in a game against Kansas City on June 20, 2004. Later that season, Rollins also hit the first inside-the-parker at San Diego's Petco Park. He had the first-ever inside-the-park home runs at two different ballparks in the same season!

46. Jim Thome had the first four–hit game at Citizens Bank Park, on April 16, 2004, vs. Montreal. The Phillies first baseman went 4–for–4 with three singles and a home run.

47. Ryan Howard had a 496–foot shot off the Marlins' Sergio Mitre that landed on Ashburn Alley on April 23, 2006. It was the first of two homers that day for Ryan, and the first multi-homer game of his career.

48. It is 409 feet in the "angle" just left of dead center field.

49. The steel and neon replica Liberty Bell in right field swings and rings.

50. They are: Robin Roberts, Richie Ashburn, Mike Schmidt, and Steve Carlton. There is also a statue of Connie Mack, which once stood outside Veterans Stadium, now located in front of the parking lot on Citizens Bank Way.

51. The bullpens are bileveled, with the opponents occupying the top bullpen and the Phillies relievers occupying the bottom pen. In the original design of the ballpark, the Phillies were in the top bullpen. But that placed them a little too close for

comfort to the rabid fans on Ashburn Alley. After the first couple of exhibition games, the Phillies pitchers decided they were better off down below. So the opponents were shifted to the top bullpen, where they would have to endure the scorn of the legendary Philly fans.

52. Baker Bowl was in North Philadelphia, at 15th and Huntingdon Streets.

53. It was called Baker Bowl after William F. Baker, who from 1913 to 1930 was the owner of the Phillies. Its original name was Philadelphia Baseball Park. Later it was called National League Park, but was usually referred to as the Huntingdon Street Grounds.

54. It was a cozy 280 feet down the right–field line. Because of that short distance, Baker Bowl was the very definition of a hitter–friendly ballpark.

55. Sheep were housed under the grandstand and would graze on the outfield and infield grass. The sheep made for a bucolic approach to groundskeeping.

56. It was Rogers Hornsby, the St. Louis Cardinals great, and one of the greatest hitters the game has ever known. A shot off Hornsby's bat broke a clubhouse window in a game in 1929.

57. The adjective "storied" gives it away, because that usually means Babe Ruth. The 40–year–old Ruth, playing for the Boston Braves, grounded out in the first inning of the first game of a doubleheader on May 30, 1935. He immediately took himself out and called it a career. It was the greatest career of all time, and it ended at Baker Bowl.

58. Twelve people were killed when the third–base grandstand collapsed during a game.

59. The fence was 60 feet high.

60. It was a once–familiar soap. The sign read, "The Phillies use Lifebuoy soap." The popular joke at the time was, "They use Lifebuoy soap, and they still stink."

61. The final game was played on June 30, 1938. The park had fallen into such disrepair that the team vacated during the middle of the season and joined the A's at Shibe.

▶ EXTRA BASE HIT

The "Vet" met its demise on March 21, 2004. Greg Luzinski pressed a ceremonial plunger to start the implosion. A crowd of fans gathered to watch and pay their last respects, while the demolition was broadcast live on all the local TV stations. The site where the stadium once stood is now a parking lot for Citizens Bank Park.

22

Whose Line Is It?

This multiple–choice quiz tests your knowledge of individual stats. Listed below are the statistical lines from individual seasons. Try to identify the player who put up those numbers.

Key: BA = batting average; H = hits; R = runs; HR = home runs; RBI = runs batted in; AB = at–bats; BB = bases on balls; SB = stolen bases; G = games; ERA = earned run average; K = strikeouts; SV = saves; 2B = doubles; 3B = triples; GS = games started; GF = games finished.

1. .305 BA, 19 HR, 66 RBI, 161 G, 637 AB, 143 R, 129 BB, 37 SB
   a. Jimmy Rollins (2007)
   b. Len Dykstra (1993)
   c. Juan Samuel (1987)

2. 286 BA, 48 HR, 121 RBI
   a. Ryan Howard (2007)
   b. Jim Thome (2003)
   c. Mike Schmidt (1980)

3. .296 BA, 30 HR, 94 RBI, 716 AB, 38 2B, 20 3B, 41 SB
   a. Jimmy Rollins (2007)
   b. Juan Samuel (1984)
   c. Bobby Abreu (2004)

4. .348 BA, 38 HR, 137 RBI, 226 H

   a. Chuck Klein (1932)
   b. Ryan Howard (2006)
   c. Ed Delahanty (1893)

5. .301 BA, 30 HR, 105 RBI, 118 R, 40 SB, 127 BB

   a. Juan Samuel (1984)
   b. Bobby Abreu (2004)
   c. Chase Utley (2006)

6. 5-7, 4.33 ERA, 3 GS, 37 GF, 21 SV

   a. Jim Konstanty (1952)
   b. Tom Gordon (2006)
   c. Brett Myers (2007)

7. .282 BA, 37 HR, 116 RBI

   a. Pat Burrell (2002)
   b. Del Ennis (1950)
   c. Mike Schmidt (1974)

8. 17-11, 2.97 ERA, 319 K

   a. Steve Carlton (1979)
   b. Robin Roberts (1958)
   c. Curt Schilling (1997)

9. .274 BA, 31 HR, 104 RBI

   a. Pat Burrell (2005)
   b. Johnny Callison (1964)
   c. Darren Daulton (1993)

10. .266 BA, 47 HR, 131 RBI, 182 K

   a. Jim Thome (2003)
   b. Mike Schmidt (1979)
   c. Greg Luzinski (1975)

ANSWERS   1.b, 2.c, 3.a, 4.a, 5.b, 6.c, 7.a, 8.c, 9.b, 10.a

23

The Nickname Game

Match the player or manager from the column on the left to his nickname found in the column on the right.

► 1

1. Darren Daulton	a. Puddin' Head
2. Von Hayes	b. Head
3. Arnold McBride	c. Styles
4. Chris Short	d. Dutch
5. Willie Jones	e. Five for One
6. Dave Hollins	f. Bake

► 2

1. Billy Hamilton	a. Crash
2. Steve Bedrosian	b. Gnat
3. Larry Bowa	c. Bedrock
4. Dick Ruthven	d. Sliding Billy
5. Dick Allen	e. Rufus

▶ **3**

1. Lenny Dykstra	a. Ol' Pete
2. Gary Matthews	b. Possum
3. Mitch Williams	c. Nails
4. George Whitted	d. Red
5. Charles Dooin	e. Sarge
6. Grover Cleveland Alexander	f. Wild Thing

▶ **4**

1. Richie Ashburn	a. Putt-Putt
2. Greg Luzinski	b. Losing Pitcher
3. Pat Moran	c. Kitty
4. Hugh Mulcahy	d. The Bull
5. Jim Kaat	e. Whiskey Face

▶ **5**

1. Tommy Greene	a. Irish
2. Mike Ryan	b. Mad Dog
3. Paul Owens	c. Cactus
4. Ryan Madson	d. Jethro
5. Gavvy Cravath	e. The Pope

▶ **6**

1. Bobby Wine	a. Hollywood
2. Steve Carlton	b. The Bat
3. Octavio Rojas	c. Wino
4. Pat Burrell	d. Lefty
5. Cole Hamels	e. Beauty
6. Dave Bancroft	f. Cookie

▶ **7**

1. Rex Hudler	a. Gramps
2. Jimmy Rollins	b. Mighty Mouse
3. Terry Francona	c. Kaiser
4. Jamie Moyer	d. Tito
5. Irving Wilhelm	e. J-Roll
6. Solly Hemus	f. Wonder Dog

▶ 8

1. Garry Maddox	a. Flyin' Hawaiian
2. Russ Meyer	b. Joe Table
3. Jose Mesa	c. Death to Flying Things
4. Pete Rose	d. Mad Monk
5. Shane Victorino	e. Secretary of Defense
6. Bob Ferguson	f. Charlie Hustle

▶ 9

1. Johnny Callison	a. Smoky
2. Dick Stuart	b. Spud
3. Forrest Burgess	c. Candy
4. Virgil Davis	d. Dr. Strangeglove
5. Bill Bransfield	e. Boom-Boom
6. Walter Beck	f. Kitty

▶ 10

1. Stan Lopata	a. Lights Out
2. Richie Ashburn	b. Chooch
3. Carlos Ruiz	c. The Hat
4. Brad Lidge	d. Big Stash
5. Gene Mauch	e. Whitey
6. Harry Walker	f. The Little General

ANSWERS **1.** 1d, 2e, 3f, 4c, 5a, 6b; **2.** 1d, 2c, 3b, 4e, 5a; **3.** 1c, 2e, 3f, 4b, 5d, 6a; **4.** 1a, 2d, 3e, 4b, 5c; **5.** 1d, 2a, 3e, 4b, 5c; **6.** 1c, 2d, 3f, 4b, 5a, 6e; **7.** 1f, 2e, 3d, 4a, 5c, 6b; **8.** 1e, 2d, 3b, 4f, 5a, 6c; **9.** 1c, 2d, 3a, 4b, 5f, 6e; **10.** 1d, 2e, 3b, 4a, 5f, 6c

24

The Numbers Game

Complete the following simple equations by using the uniform numbers of the players listed.

EXAMPLE: Larry Bowa (10) + Lenny Dykstra (4) = Pete Rose (14).

Listed below are players from the 2008 roster in addition to those players whose numbers have been retired by the Phillies.

1. Chase Utley + Mike Schmidt − Jimmy Rollins = ?

2. Ryan Howard × Pedro Feliz − Richie Ashburn = ?

3. Jayson Werth + Shane Victorino + Geoff Jenkins + Pat Burrell = ?

4. Mike Schmidt + Jim Bunning + J.C. Romero = ?

5. Robin Roberts − Chris Coste + Jimmy Rollins − Jim Bunning = ?

6. Brett Myers + Pat Burrell + Ryan Howard + Eric Bruntlett = ?

7. Adam Eaton + Chad Durbin − Chase Utley = ?

8. Mike Schmidt × Pat Burrell − Richie Ashburn = ?

9. Werth − Victorino + Utley + Howard + Rollins = ?

10. Clay Condrey ÷ Jimmy Rollins × Pedro Feliz −
    J.C. Romero = ?

More Numbers

11. Jimmy Rollins × Pat Burrell + Richie Ashburn = ?

12. Brad Lidge − Jason Werth + Tom Gordon − Brett Myers −
    Ryan Howard = ?

13. Shane Victorino × Ryan Howard − Jimmy Rollins −
    Richie Ashburn = ?

14. Ryan Madson + Pedro Feliz − Rudy Seanez + Ryan Howard
    + J.C. Romero − Jimmy Rollins + Eric Bruntlett = ?

15. Richie Ashburn + Jim Bunning + Mike Schmidt +
    Steve Carlton − Robin Roberts + Pat Burrell + Jimmy Rollins
    + Ryan Howard + Chase Utley − Cole Hamels + Brett Myers
    − Charlie Manuel + Geoff Jenkins − Jayson Werth +
    J.C. Romero − Pat Burrell + Eric Bruntlett + Pedro Feliz −
    Shane Victorino = ?

ANSWERS

1. Utley (26) + Schmidt (20) = 46 − Rollins (11)
   = **Cole Hamels (35)**

2. Howard (6) × Feliz (7) = 42 − Ashburn (1)
   = **Charlie Manuel (41)**

3. Werth (28) + Victorino (8) = 36 + Jenkins (10) = 46 +
   Burrell (5) = **Carlos Ruiz (51)**

4. Schmidt (20) + Bunning (14) = 34 + Romero (16) =
   Jamie Moyer (50)

5. Roberts (36) − Chris Coste (27) = 9 + Rollins (11) =
   20 − Bunning (14) = **Ryan Howard (6)**

6. Myers (39) + Burrell (5) = 44 + Howard (6) = 50 + Bruntlett (4) = **Brad Lidge (54)**

7. Eaton (21) + Durbin (37) = 58 − Utley (26) = **Steve Carlton (32)**

8. Schmidt (20) × Burrell (5) = 100 − Richie Ashburn (1) = **So Taguchi (99)**

9. Werth (28) − Victorino (8) = 20 + Utley (26) = 46 + Howard (6) = 52 + Rollins (11) = **Ryan Madson (63)**

10. Condrey (55) ÷ Rollins (11) = 5 × Feliz (7) = 35 − Romero (16) = **Greg Dobbs (19)**

11. Rollins (11) × Burrell (5) = 55 + Ashburn (1) = **Joe Blanton (56)**

12. Lidge (54) − Werth (28) = 26 + Gordon (45) = 71 − Myers (39) = 32 − Howard (6) = **Chase Utley (26)**

13. Victorino (8) × Howard (6) = 48 − Rollins (11) = 37 − Ashburn (1) = **Robin Roberts (36)**

14. Madson (63) + Feliz (7) = 70 − Seanez (57) = 13 + Howard (6) = 19 + Romero (16) = 35 − Rollins (11) = 24 + Bruntlett (4) = **Jayson Werth (28)**

15. Ashburn (1) + Bunning (14) + Schmidt (20) = 35 + Carlton (32) = 67 − Roberts (36) = 31 + Burrell (5) + Rollins (11) + Howard (6) = 53 + Utley (26) = 79 − Hamels (35) = 44 + Myers (39) = 83 − Manuel (41) = 42 + Jenkins (10) = 52 − Werth (28) = 24 + Romero (16) = 40 − Burrell (5) = 35 + Bruntlett (4) + Feliz (7) = 46 − Victorino (8) = **Brad Lidge (54)**

Sources

Baseball–Almanac.com

Baseball–Library.com

Baseball on the Brain, Dennis Purdy (Workman Publishing, 2007).

Baseball–Reference.com

Clearing the Bases, Mike Schmidt (HarperCollins Publishers, 2006).

The Fightin' Phils: Oddities, Insights, and Untold Stories, Rich Westcott (Camino Books, 2008).

Lost Ballparks, Lawrence S. Ritter (Viking Penguin, 1994).

The Major League Baseball Book of Fabulous Facts and Awesome Trivia, Ken Shouler (HarperCollins Publishers, 2001).

The Philadelphia Daily News

The Philadelphia Inquirer

Philadelphia Phillies 2008 Media Guide, Larry Shenk, Executive Editor.

The Phillies Encyclopedia, Third Edition, Rich Westcott and Frank Bilovsky (Temple University Press, 2004).

Phillies Essential, Rich Westcott (Triumph Books, 2006).

Sports Illustrated 2008 Sports Almanac (Sports Illustrated Books, 2007).

Wikipedia.com

Acknowledgments

I wish to remember the following people and organizations for their help and support.

First of all, many thanks to Edward Jutkowitz, publisher of Camino Books, who was willing to take a flyer on this project in the first place. I am indebted to Brad Fisher at Camino for his efforts in editing my prose and my sometimes unusual grammar and punctuation.

I am grateful to the Philadelphia Phillies, especially Greg Casterioto and Larry Shenk, and to Baseball-reference.com, a terrific website and an invaluable source of statistical information. I would also like to thank Rich Westcott, whose *Phillies Encyclopedia* proved to be a tremendous reference.

My thanks to trivia buffs Jack Scheuer and Tom Brennan for sharing their many baseball trivia questions over the years, a number of which have found their way into this book. Thanks as well to Bob Scheuer for helping to confirm a few key answers.

Lastly, but most of all, to Gina, who makes it all worthwhile.

Steve Bucci

About the Author

Steve Bucci is a television sportscaster who has covered the Phillies for the past 12 seasons. He has won the local Emmy Award for Outstanding Sports Anchor and for Best Sportscast. Bucci makes his home in Center City Philadelphia.

Champions!
A Look Back at the Phillies' Triumphant 2008 Season

By the staffs of the *Philadelphia Inquirer* and the *Philadelphia Daily News*

Featuring an outstanding set of action photos from the 2008 baseball season, this remarkable book has already become a baseball classic. Long-suffering fans who have followed the Phillies with love and passion for many years will be elated with this tribute. Sports lovers everywhere will want to join in the celebration of Philly's long-awaited World Series victory.

Eagles Facts and Trivia
Puzzlers for the Bird-Brained

John Maxymuk
with an Introduction by Ray Didinger

Through the framework of trivia questions, sports book author John Maxymuk tells many of the stories that best highlight who the Philadelphia Eagles are and why they mean so much to fans. A total of 660 tantalizing questions—covering history and rivalries, players and positions, records, the offbeat and more—will test the true fan's depth of knowledge about the Birds.

CAMINO BOOKS, INC.
P.O. Box 59026
Philadelphia, PA 19102

www.caminobooks.com

Please send me:

_____ copy(ies) of *Champions! A Look Back at the Phillies' Triumphant 2008 Season*, hardcover $24.95

_____ copy(ies) of *Eagles Facts and Trivia: Puzzlers for the Bird-Brained*, softcover $14.95

Name _____

Address _____

City/State/Zip _____

All orders must be prepaid. Your satisfaction is guaranteed. You may return the books for a full refund. Please add $5.95 for postage and handling for the first book and $1.00 for each additional.